Twice-Exceptional and Special Populations of Gifted Students

ESSENTIAL READINGS IN GIFTED EDUCATION

SERIES EDITOR

SALLY M. REIS

Susan Baum

EDITOR

TWICE-EXCEPTIONAL AND SPECIAL POPULATIONS OF GIFTED STUDENTS

A Joint Publication of Corwin Press and the National Association for Gifted Children

ESSENTIAL READINGS IN GIFTED EDUCATION
Sally M. Reis, SERIES EDITOR

CORWIN PRESS
A Sage Publications Company
Thousand Oaks, California

For information:

Corwin Press
A Sage Publications Company
2455 Teller Road
Thousand Oaks, California 91320
www.corwinpress.com

Sage Publications Ltd
1 Oliver's Yard
55 City Road
London EC1Y 1SP
United Kingdom

Sage Publications India Pvt. Ltd.
B-42, Panchsheel Enclave
Post Box 4109
New Delhi 110 017 India

Printed in the United States of America

Library of Congress Cataloging-in-Publication Data

Twice-exceptional and special populations of gifted students / Susan Baum, editor.
     p. cm. — (Essential readings in gifted education ; 7)
"A joint publication of Corwin Press and the National Association for Gifted Children."
Includes bibliographical references and index.
ISBN 1-4129-0432-3 (pbk.)
    1. Gifted children—Education—United States. 2. Students with disabilities—Education—United States. I. Baum, Susan M. II. National Association for Gifted Children (U.S.) III. Series.
LC3993.9.T95 2004
371.95—dc22
                                        2004001092

This book is printed on acid-free paper.

04 05 06 07 08 10 9 8 7 6 5 4 3 2 1

Acquisitions Editor:	Kylee Liegl
Editorial Assistant:	Jaime Cuvier
Production Editor:	Sanford Robinson
Typesetter:	C&M Digitals (P) Ltd.
Cover Designer:	Tracy E. Miller
NAGC Publications Coordinator:	Jane Clarenbach

Contents

About the Editors

Sally M. Reis is a professor and the department head of the Educational Psychology Department at the University of Connecticut where she also serves as principal investigator of the National Research Center on the Gifted and Talented. She was a teacher for 15 years, 11 of which were spent working with gifted students on the elementary, junior high, and high school levels. She has authored more than 130 articles, 9 books, 40 book chapters, and numerous monographs and technical reports.

Her research interests are related to special populations of gifted and talented students, including: students with learning disabilities, gifted females and diverse groups of talented students. She is also interested in extensions of the Schoolwide Enrichment Model for both gifted and talented students and as a way to expand offerings and provide general enrichment to identify talents and potentials in students who have not been previously identified as gifted.

She has traveled extensively conducting workshops and providing professional development for school districts on gifted education, enrichment programs, and talent development programs. She is co-author of *The Schoolwide Enrichment Model, The Secondary Triad Model, Dilemmas in Talent Development in the Middle Years*, and a book published in 1998 about women's talent development titled *Work Left Undone: Choices and Compromises of Talented Females*. Sally serves on several editorial boards, including the *Gifted Child Quarterly*, and is a past president of the National Association for Gifted Children.

Susan Baum is a professor at the College of New Rochelle where she teaches graduate courses in elementary education and the education of gifted and talented students. She received a B.S. degree in elementary and special education from Syracuse University and an M.A. degree in learning disabilities from Montclair State College. She earned a doctorate at the University of Connecticut in the education of gifted and talented. Dr. Baum has had over 30 years' experience in the public schools as a classroom teacher, special education teacher, teacher of the gifted, learning disabilities specialist, and an educational consultant.

Dr. Baum's professional activities include consulting both nationally and internationally, writing, and researching in many areas of education, including differentiated curriculum and instruction, emotional needs of children, gifted education, gifted learning disabled students, primary-aged gifted youngsters, gifted underachieving students, and economically disadvantaged students. Her publications in these areas include the following books: *Creativity 1,2,3; Chi Square, Pie Charts and Me;* and *To Be Gifted and Learning Disabled: From Identification to Practical Intervention Strategies.* She is coeditor and author of several chapters in a book titled *Nurturing the Gifts and Talents of Primary Grade Students* and is coauthor of the recent *Multiple Intelligences in the Elementary Classroom: Pathways to Thoughtful Practice,* in collaboration with Howard Gardner. Her most recent books are titled *Toolkit for Teens: A Guide for Helping Adolescents Manage Stress* and *To be Gifted & Learning Disabled: Strategies for Meeting the Needs of Gifted Students–LD, ADHD, and More* (revised edition).

Dr. Baum served on the Board of Directors of the National Association for Gifted Students and is past secretary for the organization. In addition, she is past president and founder of the Association for the Education of Gifted Underachieving Students (AEGUS).

Series Introduction

Sally M. Reis

The accomplishments of the last 50 years in the education of gifted students should not be underestimated: the field of education of the gifted and talented has emerged as strong and visible. In many states, a policy or position statement from the state board of education supports the education of the gifted and talented, and specific legislation generally recognizes the special needs of this group. Growth in our field has not been constant, however, and researchers and scholars have discussed the various high and low points of national interest and commitment to educating the gifted and talented (Gallagher, 1979; Renzulli, 1980; Tannenbaum, 1983). Gallagher described the struggle between support and apathy for special programs for gifted and talented students as having roots in historical tradition—the battle between an aristocratic elite and our concomitant belief in egalitarianism. Tannenbaum suggested the existence of two peak periods of interest in the gifted as the five years following *Sputnik* in 1957 and the last half of the decade of the 1970s, describing a valley of neglect between the peaks in which the public focused its attention on the disadvantaged and the handicapped. "The cyclical nature of interest in the gifted is probably unique in American education. No other special group of children has been alternately embraced and repelled with so much vigor by educators and laypersons alike" (Tannenbaum, 1983, p. 16). Many wonder if the cyclical nature to which Tannenbaum referred is not somewhat prophetic, as it appears that our field may be experiencing another downward spiral in interest as a result of current governmental initiatives and an increasing emphasis on testing and standardization of curriculum. Tannenbaum's description of a valley of neglect may describe current conditions. During the late 1980s, programming flourished during a peak of interest and a textbook on systems and models for gifted programs included 15 models for elementary and secondary programs (Renzulli, 1986). The Jacob Javits Gifted and Talented Students Education Act passed by Congress in 1988 resulted in the creation of the National Research Center on the Gifted and Talented, and dozens of model programs were added to the collective knowledge in the field in areas related to underrepresented populations and successful practices. In the 1990s, reduction or elimination of gifted programs occurred, as budget pressures exacerbated by the lingering recession in the late 1990s resulted in the reduction of services mandated by fewer than half of the states in our country.

Even during times in which more activity focused on the needs of gifted and talented students, concerns were still raised about the limited services provided to these students. In the second federal report on the status of education for our nation's most talented students entitled *National Excellence: A Case for Developing America's Talent* (Ross, 1993), "a quiet crisis" was described in the absence of attention paid to this population: "Despite sporadic attention over the years to the needs of bright students, most of them continue to spend time in school working well below their capabilities. The belief espoused in school reform that children from all economic and cultural backgrounds must reach their full potential has not been extended to America's most talented students. They are under-challenged and therefore underachieve" (p. 5). The report further indicates that our nation's gifted and talented students have a less rigorous curriculum, read fewer demanding books, and are less prepared for work or postsecondary education than the most talented students in many other industrialized countries. Talented children who come from economically disadvantaged homes or are members of minority groups are especially neglected, the report also indicates, and many of them will not realize their potential without some type of intervention.

In this anniversary series of volumes celebrating the evolution of our field, noted scholars introduce a collection of the most frequently cited articles from the premiere journal in our field, *Gifted Child Quarterly*. Each volume includes a collection of thoughtful, and in some cases, provocative articles that honor our past, acknowledge the challenges we face in the present, and provide hopeful guidance for the future as we seek the optimal educational experiences for all talented students. These influential articles, published after a rigorous peer review, were selected because they are frequently cited and considered seminal in our field. Considered in their entirety, the articles show that we have learned a great deal from the volume of work represented by this series. Our knowledge has expanded over several decades of work, and progress has been made toward reaching consensus about what is known. As several of the noted scholars who introduce separate areas explain in their introductions, this series helps us to understand that some questions have been answered, while others remain. While we still search for these answers, we are now better prepared to ask questions that continue and evolve. The seminal articles in this series help us to resolve some issues, while they highlight other questions that simply refuse to go away. Finally, the articles help us to identify new challenges that continue to emerge in our field. Carol Tomlinson suggests, for example, that the area of curriculum differentiation in the field of gifted education is, in her words, an issue born in the field of gifted education, and one that continues to experience rebirth.

Some of the earliest questions in our field have been answered and time has enabled those answers to be considered part of our common core of knowledge. For example, it is widely acknowledged that both school and home experiences can help to develop giftedness in persons with high potential and that a continuum of services in and out of school can provide the greatest likelihood that this development will occur. Debates over other "hot" issues such as grouping and acceleration that took place in the gifted education community 30 years ago are now largely unnecessary, as Linda Brody points out in her introduction to a series of articles in this area. General agreement seems to have been reached, for example, that grouping, enrichment and acceleration are all necessary to provide appropriate educational opportunities for gifted and talented learners. These healthy debates of the past helped to strengthen our field but visionary and reflective work remains to be done. In this series, section editors summarize what has been learned and raise provocative questions about the future. The questions alone are some of the most thoughtful in our field, providing enough research opportunities for scholars for the next decade. The brief introductions below provide some highlights about the series.

DEFINITIONS OF GIFTEDNESS (VOLUME 1)

In Volume 1, Robert Sternberg introduces us to seminal articles about definitions of giftedness and the types of talents and gifts exhibited by children and youth. The most widely used definitions of gifts and talents utilized by educators generally follow those proposed in federal reports. For example, the Marland Report (Marland, 1972) commissioned by the Congress included the first federal definition of giftedness, which was widely adopted or adapted by the states.

The selection of a definition of giftedness has been and continues to be the major policy decision made at state and local levels. It is interesting to note that policy decisions are often either unrelated or marginally related to actual procedures or to research findings about a definition of giftedness or identification of the gifted, a fact well documented by the many ineffective, incorrect, and downright ridiculous methods of identification used to find students who meet the criteria in the federal definition. This gap between policy and practice may be caused by many variables. Unfortunately, although the federal definition was written to be inclusive, it is, instead, rather vague, and problems caused by this definition have been recognized by experts in the field (Renzulli, 1978). In the most recent federal report on the status of gifted and talented programs entitled *National Excellence* (Ross, 1993), a newer federal definition is proposed based on new insights provided by neuroscience and cognitive psychology. Arguing that the term *gifted* connotes a mature power rather than a developing ability and, therefore, is antithetic to recent research findings about children, the new definition "reflects today's knowledge and thinking" (p. 26) by emphasizing talent development, stating that gifted and talented children are children and youth with outstanding talent performance or show the potential for performing at remarkably high levels of accomplishment when compared with others of their age, experience, or environment. These children and youth exhibit high performance capability in intellectual, creative, and/or artistic areas, possess an unusual leadership capacity, or excel in specific academic fields. They require services or activities not ordinarily provided by the schools. Outstanding talents are present in children and youth from all cultural groups, across all economic strata, and in all areas of human endeavor. (p. 26)

Fair identification systems use a variety of multiple assessment measures that respect diversity, accommodate students who develop at different rates, and identify potential as well as demonstrated talent. In the introduction to the volume, Sternberg admits, that just as people have bad habits, so do academic fields, explaining, "a bad habit of much of the gifted field is to do research on giftedness, or worse, identify children as gifted or not gifted, without having a clear conception of what it means to be gifted." Sternberg summarizes major themes from the seminal articles about definitions by asking key questions about the nature of giftedness and talent, the ways in which we should study giftedness, whether we should expand conventional notions of giftedness, and if so, how that can be accomplished; whether differences exist between giftedness and talent; the validity of available assessments; and perhaps most importantly, how do we and can we develop giftedness and talent. Sternberg succinctly summarizes points of broad agreement from the many scholars who have contributed to this section, concluding that giftedness involves more than just high IQ, that it has noncognitive and cognitive components, that the environment is crucial in terms of whether potentials for gifted performance will be realized, and that giftedness is not a single thing. He further cautions that the ways we conceptualize giftedness greatly influences who will have opportunities to develop their gifts and reminds readers of our responsibilities as educators. He also asks one of the most critical questions in our field: whether gifted and talented individuals will use their knowledge to benefit or harm our world.

IDENTIFICATION OF HIGH-ABILITY STUDENTS (VOLUME 2)

In Volume 2, Joseph Renzulli introduces what is perhaps the most critical question still facing practitioners and researchers in our field, that is how, when, and why should we identify gifted and talented students. Renzulli believes that conceptions of giftedness exist along a continuum ranging from a very conservative or restricted view of giftedness to a more flexible or multidimensional approach. What many seem not to understand is that the first step in identification should always be to ask: identification for what? For what type of program or experience is the youngster being identified? If, for example, an arts program is being developed for talented artists, the resulting identification system must be structured to identify youngsters with either demonstrated or potential talent in art.

Renzulli's introductory chapter summarizes seminal articles about identification, and summarizes emerging consensus. For example, most suggest, that while intelligence tests and other cognitive ability tests provide one very important form of information about one dimension of a young person's potential, mainly in the areas of verbal and analytic skills, they do not tell us all that we need to know about who should be identified. These authors do not argue that cognitive ability tests should be dropped from the identification process. Rather, most believe that (a) other indicators of potential should be used for identification, (b) these indicators should be given equal consideration when it comes to making final decisions about which students will be candidates for special services, and (c) in the final analysis, it is the thoughtful judgment of knowledgeable professionals rather than instruments and cutoff scores that should guide selection decisions.

Another issue addressed by the authors of the seminal articles about identification is what has been referred to as the distinction between (a) convergent and divergent thinking (Guilford, 1967; Torrance, 1984), (b) entrenchment and non-entrenchment (Sternberg, 1982), and (c) schoolhouse giftedness versus creative/productive giftedness (Renzulli, 1982; Renzulli & Delcourt, 1986). It is easier to identify schoolhouse giftedness than it is to identify students with the potential for creative productive giftedness. Renzulli believes that progress has been made in the identification of gifted students, especially during the past quarter century, and that new approaches address the equity issue, policies, and practices that respect new theories about human potential and conceptions of giftedness. He also believes, however, that continuous commitment to research-based identification practices is still needed, for "it is important to keep in mind that some of the characteristics that have led to the recognition of history's most gifted contributors are not always as measurable as others. We need to continue our search for those elusive things that are left over after everything explainable has been explained, to realize that giftedness is culturally and contextually imbedded in all human activity, and most of all, to value the value of even those things that we cannot yet explain."

ACCELERATION AND GROUPING, CURRICULUM, AND CURRICULUM DIFFERENTIATION (VOLUMES 3, 4, 5)

Three volumes in this series address curricular and grouping issues in gifted programs, and it is in this area, perhaps, that some of the most promising practices have been implemented for gifted and talented students. Grouping and curriculum interact with each other, as various forms of grouping patterns have enabled students to work on advanced curricular opportunities with other talented students. And, as is commonly known now about instructional and ability grouping, it is not the way students are grouped that matters most, but rather, it is what happens within the groups that makes the most difference.

In too many school settings, little differentiation of curriculum and instruction for gifted students is provided during the school day, and minimal opportunities are offered. Occasionally, after-school enrichment programs or Saturday programs offered by museums, science centers, or local universities take the place of comprehensive school programs, and too many academically talented students attend school in classrooms across the country in which they are bored, unmotivated, and unchallenged. Acceleration, once a frequently used educational practice in our country, is often dismissed by teachers and administrators as an inappropriate practice for a variety of reasons, including scheduling problems, concerns about the social effects of grade skipping, and others. Various forms of acceleration, including enabling precocious students to enter kindergarten or first grade early, grade skipping, and early entrance to college are not commonly used by most school districts.

Unfortunately, major alternative grouping strategies involve the reorganization of school structures, and these have been too slow in coming, perhaps due to the difficulty of making major educational changes, because of scheduling, finances, and other issues that have caused schools to substantially delay major change patterns. Because of this delay, gifted students too often fail to receive classroom instruction based on their unique needs that place them far ahead of their chronological peers in basic skills and verbal abilities and enable them to learn much more rapidly and tackle much more complex materials than their peers. Our most able students need appropriately paced, rich and challenging instruction, and curriculum that varies significantly from what is being taught in regular classrooms across America. Too often, academically talented students are "left behind" in school.

Linda Brody introduces the question of how to group students optimally for instructional purposes and pays particular concern to the degree to which the typical age-in-grade instructional program can meet the needs of gifted students—those students with advanced cognitive abilities and achievement that may already have mastered the curriculum designed for their age peers. The articles about grouping emphasize the importance of responding to the learning needs of individual students with curricular flexibility, the need for educators to be flexible when assigning students to instructional groups, and the need to modify those groups when necessary. Brody's introduction points out that the debate about grouping gifted and talented learners together was one area that brought the field together, as every researcher in the field supports some type of grouping option, and few would disagree with the need to use grouping and accelerated learning as tools that allow us to differentiate content for students with different learning needs. When utilized as a way to offer a more advanced educational program to students with advanced cognitive abilities and achievement levels, these practices can help achieve the goal of an appropriate education for all students.

Joyce VanTassel-Baska introduces the seminal articles in curriculum, by explaining that they represent several big ideas that emphasize the values and relevant factors of a curriculum for the gifted, the technology of curriculum development, aspects of differentiation of a curriculum for the gifted within core subject areas and without, and the research-based efficacy of such curriculum and related instructional pedagogy in use. She also reminds readers of Harry Passow's concerns about curriculum balance, suggesting that an imbalance exists, as little evidence suggests that the affective development of gifted students is occurring through special curricula for the gifted. Moreover, interdisciplinary efforts at curriculum frequently exclude the arts and foreign language. Only through acknowledging and applying curriculum balance in these areas are we likely to be producing the type of humane individual Passow envisioned. To achieve balance, VanTassel-Baska recommends a full set of curriculum options across domains, as well as the need to nurture the social-emotional needs of diverse gifted and talented learners.

Carol Tomlinson introduces the critical area of differentiation in the field of gifted education that has only emerged in the last 13 years. She believes the diverse nature of the articles and their relatively recent publication suggests that this area is indeed, in her words, "an issue born in the field of gifted education, and one that continues to experience rebirth." She suggests that one helpful way of thinking about the articles in this volume is that their approach varies, as some approach the topic of differentiation of curriculum with a greater emphasis on the distinctive mission of gifted education. Others look at differentiation with a greater emphasis on the goals, issues, and missions shared between general education and gifted education. Drawing from an analogy with anthropology, Tomlinson suggests that "splitters" in that field focus on differences among cultures while "lumpers" have a greater interest in what cultures share in common. Splitters ask the question of what happens for high-ability students in mixed-ability settings, while lumpers question what common issues and solutions exist for multiple populations in mixed-ability settings.

Tomlinson suggests that the most compelling feature of the collection of articles in this section—and certainly its key unifying feature—is the linkage between the two areas of educational practice in attempting to address an issue likely to be seminal to the success of both over the coming quarter century and beyond, and this collection may serve as a catalyst for next steps in those directions for the field of gifted education as it continues collaboration with general education and other educational specialties while simultaneously addressing those missions uniquely its own.

UNDERREPRESENTED AND TWICE-EXCEPTIONAL POPULATIONS AND SOCIAL AND EMOTIONAL ISSUES (VOLUMES 6, 7, 8)

The majority of young people participating in gifted and talented programs across the country continue to represent the majority culture in our society. Few doubts exist regarding the reasons that economically disadvantaged, twice-exceptional, and culturally diverse students are underrepresented in gifted programs. One reason may be the ineffective and inappropriate identification and selection procedures used for the identification of these young people that limits referrals and nominations and eventual placement. Research summarized in this series indicates that groups that have been traditionally underrepresented in gifted programs could be better served if some of the following elements are considered: new constructs of giftedness, attention to cultural and contextual variability, the use of more varied and authentic assessments, performance-based identification, and identification opportunities through rich and varied learning opportunities.

Alexinia Baldwin discusses the lower participation of culturally diverse and underserved populations in programs for the gifted as a major concern that has forged dialogues and discussion in *Gifted Child Quarterly* over the past five decades. She classifies these concerns in three major themes: *identification/selection, programming,* and *staff assignment and development.* Calling the first theme **Identification/Selection**, she indicates that it has always been the Achilles' heel of educators' efforts to ensure that giftedness can be expressed in many ways through broad identification techniques. Citing favorable early work by Renzulli and Hartman (1971) and Baldwin (1977) that expanded options for identification, Baldwin cautions that much remains to be done. The second theme, **Programming**, recognizes the abilities of students who are culturally diverse but often forces them to exist in programs designed "for one size fits all." Her third theme relates to **Staffing and Research,** as she voices concerns about the diversity of teachers in these programs as well as the attitudes or mindsets of researchers who develop theories and conduct the research that addresses these concerns.

Susan Baum traces the historical roots of gifted and talented individuals with special needs, summarizing Terman's early work that suggested the gifted were healthier, more popular, and better adjusted than their less able peers. More importantly, gifted individuals were regarded as those who could perform at high levels in all areas with little or no support. Baum suggests that acceptance of these stereotypical characteristics diminished the possibility that there could be special populations of gifted students with special needs. Baum believes that the seminal articles in this collection address one or more of the critical issues that face gifted students at risk and suggest strategies for overcoming the barriers that prevent them from realizing their promise. The articles focus on three populations of students: twice-exceptional students—gifted students who are at risk for poor development due to difficulties in learning and attention;

gifted students who face gender issues that inhibit their ability to achieve or develop socially and emotionally, and students who are economically disadvantaged and at risk for dropping out of school. Baum summarizes research indicating that each of these groups of youngsters is affected by one or more barriers to development, and the most poignant of these barriers are identification strategies, lack of awareness of consequences of co-morbidity, deficit thinking in program design, and lack of appropriate social and emotional support. She ends her introduction with a series of thoughtful questions focusing on future directions in this critical area.

Sidney Moon introduces the seminal articles on the social and emotional development of and counseling for gifted children by acknowledging the contributions of the National Association for Gifted Children's task forces that have examined social/emotional issues. The first task force, formed in 2000 and called the Social and Emotional Issues Task Force, completed its work in 2002 by publishing an edited book, *The Social and Emotional Development of Gifted Children: What Do We Know?* This volume provides an extensive review of the literature on the social and emotional development of gifted children (Neihart, Reis, Robinson, & Moon, 2002). Moon believes that the seminal studies in the area of the social and emotional development and counseling illustrate both the strengths and the weaknesses of the current literature on social and emotional issues in the field of gifted education. These articles bring increased attention to the affective needs of special populations of gifted students, such as underachievers, who are at risk for failure to achieve their potential, but also point to the need for more empirical studies on "what works" with these students, both in terms of preventative strategies and more intensive interventions. She acknowledges that although good counseling models have been developed, they need to be rigorously evaluated to determine their effectiveness under disparate conditions, and calls for additional research on the affective and counseling interventions with specific subtypes of gifted students such as Asian Americans, African Americans, and twice-exceptional students. Moon also strongly encourages researchers in the field of gifted education to collaborate with researchers from affective fields such as personal and social psychology, counseling psychology, family therapy, and psychiatry to learn to intervene most effectively with gifted individuals with problems and to learn better how to help all gifted persons achieve optimal social, emotional, and personal development.

ARTISTICALLY AND CREATIVELY TALENTED STUDENTS (VOLUMES 9, 10)

Enid Zimmerman introduces the volume on talent development in the visual and performing arts with a summary of articles about students who are talented in music, dance, visual arts, and spatial, kinesthetic, and expressive areas. Major themes that appear in the articles include perceptions by parents, students, and teachers that often focus on concerns related to nature versus nurture in arts talent development; research about the crystallizing experiences of artistically talented students; collaboration between school and community members about identification of talented art students from diverse backgrounds; and leadership issues related to empowering teachers of talented arts students. They all are concerned to some extent with teacher, parent, and student views about educating artistically talented students. Included also are discussions about identification of talented students from urban, suburban, and rural environments. Zimmerman believes that in this particular area, a critical need exists for research about the impact of educational opportunities, educational settings, and the role of art teachers on the development of artistically talented students. The impact of the standards and testing movement and its relationship to the education of talented students in the visual and performing arts is an area greatly in need of investigation. Research also is needed about students' backgrounds, personalities, gender orientations, skill development, and cognitive and affective abilities as well as cross-cultural contexts and the impact of global and popular culture on the education of artistically talented students. The compelling case study with which she introduces this volume sets the stage for the need for this research.

Donald Treffinger introduces reflections on articles about creativity by discussing the following five core themes that express the collective efforts of researchers to grasp common conceptual and theoretical challenges associated with creativity. The themes include **Definitions** (how we define giftedness, talent, or creativity), **Characteristics** (the indicators of giftedness and creativity in people), **Justification** (Why is creativity important in education?), **Assessment** of creativity, and the ways we **Nurture** creativity. Treffinger also discusses the expansion of knowledge, the changes that have occurred, the search for answers, and the questions that still remain. In the early years of interest of creativity research, Treffinger believed that considerable discussion existed about whether it was possible to foster creativity through training or instruction. He reports that over the last 50 years, educators have learned that deliberate efforts to nurture creativity are possible (e.g., Torrance, 1987), and further extends this line of inquiry by asking the key question, "What works best, for whom, and under what conditions?" Treffinger summarizes the challenges faced by educators who try to nurture the development of creativity through effective teaching and to ask which experiences will have the greatest impact, as these will help to determine our ongoing lines of research, development, and training initiatives.

EVALUATION AND PUBLIC POLICY (VOLUMES 11, 12)

Carolyn Callahan introduces the seminal articles on evaluation and suggests that this important component neglected by experts in the field of gifted education for at least the last three decades can be a plea for important work by both evaluators and practitioners. She divides the seminal literature on evaluation, and in particular the literature on the evaluation of gifted programs into four categories, those which (a) provide theory and/or practical guidelines, (b) describe or report on specific program evaluations, (c) provide stimuli for the discussion of issues surrounding the evaluation process, and (d) suggest new research on the evaluation process. Callahan concludes with a challenge indicating work to be done and the opportunity for experts to make valuable contributions to increased effectiveness and efficiency of programs for the gifted.

James Gallagher provides a call-to-arms in the seminal articles he introduces on public policy by raising some of the most challenging questions in the field. Gallagher suggests that as a field, we need to come to some consensus about stronger interventions and consider how we react to accusations of elitism. He believes that our field could be doing a great deal more with additional targeted resources supporting the general education teacher and the development of specialists in gifted education, and summarizes that our failure to fight in the public arena for scarce resources may raise again the question posed two decades ago by Renzulli (1980), looking toward 1990: "Will the gifted child movement be alive and well in 2010?"

CONCLUSION

What can we learn from an examination of our field and the seminal articles that have emerged over the last few decades? First, we must **respect the past** by acknowledging the times in which articles were written and the shoulders of those persons upon whom we stand as we continue to create and develop our field. An old proverb tells us that when we drink from the well, we must remember to acknowledge those who dug the well, and in our field the early articles represent the seeds that grew our field. Next, we must **celebrate the present** and the exciting work and new directions in our field and the knowledge that is now accepted as a common core. Last, we must **embrace the future** by understanding that there is no finished product when it comes to research on gifted and talented children and how we are best able to meet their unique needs. Opportunities abound in the work reported in this series, but many questions remain. A few things seem clear. Action in the future should be based on both qualitative and quantitative research as well as longitudinal studies, and what we have completed only scratches the surface regarding the many variables and issues that still need to be explored. Research is needed that suggests positive changes that will lead to more inclusive programs that recognize the talents and gifts of diverse students in our country. When this occurs, future teachers and researchers in gifted education will find answers that can be embraced by educators, communities, and families, and the needs of all talented and gifted students will be more effectively met in their classrooms by teachers who have been trained to develop their students' gifts and talents.

We also need to consider carefully how we work with the field of education in general. As technology emerges and improves, new opportunities will become available to us. Soon, all students should be able to have their curricular needs preassessed before they begin any new curriculum unit. Soon, the issue of keeping students on grade-level material when they are many grades ahead should disappear as technology enables us to pinpoint students' strengths. Will chronological grades be eliminated? The choices we have when technology enables us to learn better what students already know presents exciting scenarios for the future, and it is imperative that we advocate carefully for multiple opportunities for these students, based on their strengths and interests, as well as a challenging core curriculum. Parents, educators, and professionals who care about these special populations need to become politically active to draw attention to the unique needs of these students, and researchers need to conduct the experimental studies that can prove the efficacy of providing talent development options as well as opportunities for healthy social and emotional growth.

For any field to continue to be vibrant and to grow, new voices must be heard, and new players sought. A great opportunity is available in our field; for as we continue to advocate for gifted and talented students, we can also play important roles in the changing educational reform movement. We can continue to work to achieve more challenging opportunities for all students while we fight to maintain gifted, talented, and enrichment programs. We can continue our advocacy for differentiation through acceleration, individual curriculum opportunities, and a continuum of advanced curriculum and personal support opportunities. The questions answered and those raised in this volume of seminal articles can help us to move forward as a field. We hope those who read the series will join us in this exciting journey.

REFERENCES

Baldwin, A.Y. (1977). Tests do underpredict: A case study. *Phi Delta Kappan, 58,* 620-621.

Gallagher, J. J. (1979). Issues in education for the gifted. In A. H. Passow (Ed.), *The gifted and the talented: Their education and development* (pp. 28-44). Chicago: University of Chicago Press.

Guilford, J. E. (1967). *The nature of human intelligence.* New York: McGraw-Hill.

Marland, S. P., Jr. (1972). *Education of the gifted and talented: Vol. 1. Report to the Congress of the United States by the U.S. Commissioner of Education.* Washington, DC: U.S. Government Printing Office.

Neihart, M., Reis, S., Robinson, N., & Moon, S. M. (Eds.). (2002). *The social and emotional development of gifted children: What do we know?* Waco, TX: Prufrock.

Renzulli, J. S. (1978). What makes giftedness? Reexamining a definition. *Phi Delta Kappan, 60*(5), 180-184.

Renzulli, J. S. (1980). Will the gifted child movement be alive and well in 1990? *Gifted Child Quarterly, 24*(1), 3-9. **[See Vol. 12.]**

Renzulli, J. (1982). Dear Mr. and Mrs. Copernicus: We regret to inform you . . . *Gifted Child Quarterly, 26*(1), 11-14. **[See Vol. 2.]**

Renzulli, J. S. (Ed.). (1986). *Systems and models for developing programs for the gifted and talented.* Mansfield Center, CT: Creative Learning Press.

Renzulli, J. S., & Delcourt, M. A. B. (1986). The legacy and logic of research on the identification of gifted persons. *Gifted Child Quarterly, 30*(1), 20-23. **[See Vol. 2.]**

Renzulli J., & Hartman, R. (1971). Scale for rating behavioral characteristics of superior students. *Exceptional Children, 38,* 243-248.

Ross, P. (1993). *National excellence: A case for developing America's talent.* Washington, DC: U.S. Department of Education, Government Printing Office.

Sternberg, R. J. (1982). Nonentrenchment in the assessment of intellectual giftedness. *Gifted Child Quarterly, 26*(2), 63-67. **[See Vol. 2.]**

Tannenbaum, A. J. (1983). *Gifted children: Psychological and educational perspectives.* New York: Macmillan.

Torrance, E. P. (1984). The role of creativity in identification of the gifted and talented. *Gifted Child Quarterly, 28*(4), 153-156. **[See Vols. 2 and 10.]**

Torrance, E. P. (1987). Recent trends in teaching children and adults to think creatively. In S. G. Isaksen (Ed.), *Frontiers of creativity research: Beyond the basics* (pp. 204-215). Buffalo, NY: Bearly Limited.

Introduction to Twice-Exceptional and Special Populations of Gifted Students

Susan Baum

College of New Rochelle

Since the publication of the volumes of the *Genetic Studies of Genius* (Terman, 1925; Terman & Oden, 1947; Sears, 1979) many have defined gifted individuals solely as those who had superior intelligence as measured by an IQ test. Such individuals were thought to be healthier, more popular, and better adjusted than their less able peers. More importantly, gifted individuals were those who could perform at high levels in all areas with little or no support. Acceptance of these stereotypical characteristics greatly diminished the possibility that there could be special populations of gifted students who were not "practically perfect in every way." Entertaining the idea that someone could be gifted if they could not read, for instance, was irresponsible. The consideration that giftedness could be masked by gender, cultural, economic, or behavioral issues was similarly irrational.

With broadened definitions of giftedness promoted by researchers such as Renzulli (1978), Sternberg (1986) and Gardner (1983) as well as the birth of a federal definition of giftedness in 1978, the possibility of identifying gifted students from special populations became both plausible and promising. Seminal work by Joanne Whitmore (1980) and June Maker (1977) introduced the idea that students with special needs could indeed be gifted. About the same time Alexinia Baldwin (1978) and Mary Frasier (1980) were alerting the field to the issues of giftedness among the ethnically diverse and economically disadvantaged youth. Since then, many concerned experts in the field of gifted education have turned their attention to special populations of students who have been typically underrepresented in gifted programs or whose needs have not been recognized or met. In 1988 Congress saw the need to promote the interests of gifted and talented especially those from at-risk special populations—economically disadvantaged, students with special needs, and students with limited English proficiency. To this end, Congress passed the Jacob Javits Gifted and Talented Students Education Act that has allocated millions of dollars to both researching the needs of these youngsters and developing means of reversing the increasing trend of inequity and lack of access to gifted programs.

Unfortunately, the increased attention has met with limited success in providing comprehensive programs for students who are gifted but challenged in some ways. (Baum & Owen, in press; Grantham, 2002). Not only are these populations at great risk for appropriate services but the number of categories of gifted students with challenges is multiplying. For instance, gender inequities i.e., gifted females, gifted males, and gay and lesbian students are a growing concern. Although much has been learned about the social and emotional issues that may impede the development of potential for these gifted students, services for these students are minimal. Additionally, special educators are finding giftedness among students who, until recently, have not been mentioned in the literature, i.e., gifted students with Asperger's Syndrome, Attention Deficit Disorder (ADD), Oppositional Defiant Disorder, or Pervasive Developmental Disorders otherwise unspecified. Each new group of special populations manifests unique needs and requires complex solutions.

ISSUES FACING GIFTED CHILDREN FROM SPECIAL POPULATIONS

Far too many nontraditional gifted youngsters continue to be underrepresented in programs for gifted and talented. These youngsters often do not meet identification criteria or are considered for remedial services. Even though the research concerning the needs of these youngsters is considerable, these students lack appropriate interventions and programs. The *Gifted Child Quarterly* articles represented in this collection address one or more of the critical issues that face gifted students at risk, and suggest strategies for overcoming the barriers that prevent them from realizing their promise. The articles focus on three populations of students: twice-exceptional students—gifted students who are at risk for development due to difficulties in learning and attention; gifted students whose gender issues inhibit their ability to achieve or develop socially and emotionally; and students who are economically disadvantaged and at risk for dropping out of school. One or more barriers to development affect each of these groups of youngsters. The most poignant of these barriers are identification strategies, lack of awareness of consequences of co-morbidity, deficit thinking in program design, and lack of appropriate social and emotional support. (Baum & Owen, in press; Chae, Kim, & Sun Noh, 2003; Ford, Harris, Tyson, & Trotman, 2002; Tomlinson, Callahan, & Lelli, 1997). The following questions tap into these barriers.

How can we identify gifted potential in nontraditional students? Special learning needs, cultural expectations, and issues of poverty greatly complicate the identification of gifts and talents among at-risk students. Traditional measures may not be reliable or valid for these special populations. Learning traits that are indicative of advanced abilities and creativity may manifest themselves negatively. Also, a lack of experiences and resources may depress cognitive development resulting in low or depressed scores on standardized tests. Traditional testing is not sensitive to these individual differences. Consequently, results can erroneously omit many youngsters with high levels of talent or academic potential from being identified as gifted. Several of the authors describe the challenge of identification and suggest strategies for improving identification through the use of nontraditional and more authentic strategies. (Baum, 1988; Baum, Olenchak, & Owen, 1997; Neihart, 2000; Spicker, Southern, & Davis, 1987).

How does co-morbidity challenge traditional methods of intervention? Lack of understanding of the consequences of two diverse sets of traits obscures identification and often contributes to inappropriate diagnosis and programming. Researchers have supported the idea that gifted students from special populations have needs that are different from their more traditional gifted peers and from peers with similar challenges (Baum & Olenchak, 2002; Bernal, 2002). These special gifted youngsters have unique needs and require interventions that speak to both their gift and their challenge. Too often, one trait can disguise the other. Or worse, the lack of recognition of all facets of the circumstance can elicit complications far different than the issues attributed to one or the other trait. Ignorance of the duality of characteristics has led to underidentification as well as misdiagnoses. This theme is explored in several of the included articles (Baum, Olenchak, & Owen, 1998; Neihart, 2000; Peterson & Rischar, 2000; Reis, 1987; Spicker, Southern, & Davis, 1987).

How do we design comprehensive programs for special populations of gifted students that go beyond deficit thinking? Because prevailing policies focus on remediation, gifted students with poor learning strategies, behavioral difficulties, or academic deficits may not be considered for talent development but instead be placed in restrictive environments that focus on deficits. Many of the included articles describe the characteristics of particular special populations of gifted students and suggest promising practices in response to a lack of appropriate programs to address the needs of these youngsters. These approaches incorporate talent development where skills in self-regulation and compensation are provided within the context of challenging and enriched curricula (Baum, 1988; Neihart, 2000; Reis, 1987; Reis, McGuire, & Neu, 2000; Renzulli & Park, 2000; Spicker, Southern, & Davis, 1987).

Is counseling support needed for gifted students to cope with cultural and environmental influences or biases that negatively impact their development? Several articles in this collection reveal social and emotional concomitants of the coincidence of giftedness and other more debilitating characteristics. The authors identify issues of lack of self-efficacy, poor self-regulation and motivation, depression, low self-esteem, underachievement, and depression to be severe among this population of students. These authors promote focused attention to the social and emotional needs of these youngsters and suggest specific strategies including the need for professional counseling. (Baum, Olenchak, & Owen, 1998; Peterson, & Rischar, 2000; Reis, 1987; Renzulli & Park, 2000).

MANIFESTATION OF ISSUES FOR GIFTED STUDENTS WITHIN SPECIFIC POPULATIONS

Each of these barriers has a unique relationship to the three populations of students targeted in this collection of articles: twice-exceptional students, students with gender-related issues, and economically disadvantaged students. The following section summarizes the issues for each population and provides a summary of the authors' ideas, concerns, and suggestions.

Twice-Exceptional Students

The first set of articles focuses on students who are twice exceptional. Like many gifted students these youngsters are highly knowledgeable and have talents in particular areas. They can think critically, pursue topics, and create solutions to problems. However, these same youngsters often are overwhelmed by special learning difficulties that thwart their development and obscure their gifted potential. Faced by educational practices and policies that may confuse and complicate appropriate diagnosis coupled with the prevailing emphasis on remediation over talent development, programs for these students are often inappropriate or lacking (Baum & Olenchak, 2002). Further exacerbating the issue is a general ignorance of the social and emotional implications of the coincidence of giftedness and specific disabilities.

Two articles emphasize the needs of students who are both gifted and learning disabled. Baum (1988) explores the necessity of identifying and nurturing students' gifts and talents at the elementary level. The article evaluates the results of an enrichment program designed to meet the dual needs of these youngsters. The program, based on the *Enrichment Triad Model*, resulted in students improving in both self-regulation and achievement. When students were allowed to pursue and create in areas of interest, they were willing to put forth time and effort to create high-level products. During the course of their creative pursuits, they learned compensation strategies such as time management, organization, and ways to communicate that aligned with their strengths.

Reis, McGuire, and Neu (2000) extend this theme with their presentation of the results of a qualitative study focusing on the strategies bright students with learning disabilities use to achieve success at the university level. These students all attended a program at the university designed to assist students with learning disabilities. This program provided essential support to students including offering appropriate compensation strategies to offset problematic deficits. The findings of the study indicate that these students had not learned compensation strategies in their special education programs during elementary and high school years, nor, in most cases, were they involved in gifted programs. Thus, they had extremely negative attitudes about school. Through their participation in the university program they found multiple strategies that worked for them and developed their ability to focus on their talents rather than being overwhelmed by their deficits. The authors suggest that programs for gifted students with learning disabilities focus on teaching self-regulation rather than remediation.

Another population of twice-exceptional children is students who are gifted and creative but are simultaneously hampered with attention difficulties. Baum, Olenchak, and Owen, (1998) explore the issues surrounding the coincidence of ADHD and giftedness. This dual classification has been increasing in recent years causing some concern about a possible overidentification of ADHD among gifted students. This may be due to delicate interaction between characteristics of gifted or creative students and the demands of the learning environment. The article suggests that in some cases the environment for gifted students can be somewhat hostile, exacerbating the appearance of ADHD-like behaviors. One example is teachers' reluctance to adapt to the pace and depth of learning for gifted students. This article provides guidelines and approaches for determining appropriate diagnosis and offers suggestions for helping these twice-exceptional youngsters succeed. Again, appropriate diagnosis will depend on first assuring that the learning environment aligns to the students' gifts and talents.

Another twice-exceptional population of gifted students that is drawing attention is gifted students with Asperger's Syndrome. Neihart (2000) discusses appropriate diagnosis of this special group of youngsters. She posits that these students may appear like highly gifted children who are a bit "quirky." She suggests that their behavior, however, can be confused with learning disabilities or attention deficits precluding appropriate diagnosis and appropriate interventions. Neihart presents typical characteristics of students with Asperger's Syndrome and distinguishes them from gifted behaviors. Neihart concludes that these students, like learning disabled students, benefit greatly from social skills training and other kinds of strategies that will help them to compensate for learning difficulties. Finally, similar to the needs of all twice-exceptional youngsters, these individuals with the appropriate support can rise to eminence because of their exceptional gifts and talents.

Gifted Students With Gender Issues

The next set of articles targets gender issues that contribute to the under-achievement of gifted females and the perilous journey of development for students who are both gifted and gay. Unlike the students who are twice excep-tional, where their disabilities in learning may impede their development, these gifted youngsters are thwarted by the social and emotional milieu (Reis, 1987). The special challenge faced by both gifted girls and the gay population is to forge a trail to success through unfriendly environments where expectations favor gifted straight males in subtle and not so subtle ways.

Reis (1987, 1998) describes the factors contributing to the underachievement of gifted females and suggests that underachievement for gifted girls can be regarded as a failure to meet expectations in school and later in life. For gifted women, underachievement may equate with an inability to reach professional benchmarks set by men in myriad professions or the perception that achieve-ment, as defined by men, equates with successful careers, without taking into account that giftedness in women may need to be redefined. Inappropriate standards provide inappropriate comparisons. She identifies cultural stereo-typing, fear of success, lack of planning, perfectionism, and the need to priori-tize goals in accordance with values as contributing factors to a pattern of underachievement in women of high potential. The article concludes with the call for future research to define the specific emotional, social, and cultural influences affecting achievement and happiness for gifted females so that appropriate interventions and guidance programs can be provided.

Peterson and Rischar (2000) summarize some of the challenges faced by students who are gifted and gay and describe the emotional turmoil faced by these young people whom they describe as "doubly different" (p. 241). The world is particularly hostile for these youngsters. First admitting their sexual preferences to self and others is extremely difficult. They may find no safe haven where they can explore their feelings in a nonjudgmental forum. Next, their giftedness itself can make them even more sensitive to the trials and tribu-lations they must face to find peace. In a qualitative study with 18 gifted young adults who identify themselves as being gay/lesbian/bisexual, the authors found that these students feel alienated and marginalized by both their gifted-ness and sexual orientation. They describe mostly negative school experiences where the attitudes of both teachers and peers were hurtful. They admitted to severe depression and thoughts of self-destructive behavior. Peterson and Rischar (2000) explain how sexual development identity may impact normal development in other areas. The article concludes with specific strategies for aid-ing these students in accepting and acknowledging who they are and for estab-lishing a school climate of acceptance, compassion, and appreciation of diversity.

Economically Disadvantaged Gifted Students

Many populations of gifted students are thwarted in their development because of poverty and lack of experiences (Oreck, Baum, & McCartney, 2000;

Slocum & Payne, 2000). The final set of articles examines economic influences on personal development. Rural and urban students are included. The first article examines the issue of identifying gifted students from poor rural areas; the second targets the population of gifted dropouts. While there are a multitude of issues surrounding both these situations, chief among them are economic factors.

Spicker, Southern, and Davis (1987) discuss the effects of rural living, sparse populations, poverty, non-urban acculturation, experiences and traditional values that impact both identification of gifted youngsters and finding the resources to develop their gifts and talents. They explain that the problem of poverty often impedes development of children with respect to language, perception, curiosity, and self-efficacy. Issues of poverty also interfere with the youngsters building healthy attitudes about school and learning. These factors contribute to the impoverished students' inability to fare well on standardized tests of ability or achievement. Even if these students are identified as gifted, lack of resources and support by the family and school challenges the development of the gifts and talents of these special youngsters. Spicker, Southern, and Davis (1987) conclude by suggesting strategies for counteracting these difficulties. Some examples include using alternate identification procedures, increasing teacher awareness of the nature and needs of this population, locating community resources, and connecting with other districts to share resources and link students to appropriate peers.

The greatest risk economically disadvantaged gifted students both rural and urban face is the failure to complete school and develop their potential. In the final article, Renzulli and Park (2000) argue that a major characteristic of the gifted dropout population is poverty. The authors claim that gifted students who drop out of school most often came from families with low social economic status and had parents with low levels of education. In addition, gifted dropouts tended not to participate in extracurricular activities, had low educational aspirations, and left school primarily for school-related or personal problems. Most of these youngsters did not like school, were failing, or had personal problems that required their attention like being pregnant or having to work. The authors recommend that schools and teachers need to identify potential gifted dropouts in the early grades so that they can provide challenging curriculum that aligns to students' strengths, styles, and interests. Schools need to provide enriched opportunities, counseling services, and opportunities for communicating with the families.

NEEDS, CHALLENGES, AND QUESTIONS TO PONDER

While each group presents unique issues, general themes repeat themselves as essential ingredients of providing appropriate services for the "doubly different" (Peterson & Rischar, 2000, p. 241). In other words, to effectively help students with two sets of needs (which at times may seem to conflict with each other) we may need to dually differentiate their experiences (Baum, Cooper, & Neu, 2001). On the one hand, we must remember that these students are gifted and need experiences to challenge their gifts. But at the same time, their unique situations may require modifications, accommodations, and additional services to nurture their academic, social, and emotional development. The following provides an overview of common needs facing gifted students at risk. The questions below each alert us to the challenges we must confront if we are to provide appropriate educational experiences for these special populations of gifted students.

Issue 1: These students require talent development experiences.

- Are the definitions of giftedness sufficiently broad to include these populations?
- Are identification strategies valid for the population?
- Are all talents valued and allowed expression?
- Are there sufficient resources to nurture the talent?

Issue 2: These students deserve learning environments that support their academic, social, and emotional needs.

- Are the students appropriately challenged in the regular classroom?
- Are they being taught in ways that accentuate their learning differences and styles?
- Have students been appropriately diagnosed for any learning needs?
- Have appropriate accommodations or modifications been provided?
- Are there opportunities to learn self-regulation strategies?
- Do the students have experiences with peers of similar issues and abilities?
- Are there appropriate counseling opportunities where students can explore their unique issues?
- Are there role models or mentors for these students with whom they can identify?

Issue 3: The families of these students should be aware of the unique needs of their children and how to meet them.

- Are there parent support groups?
- Are parents made aware of the unique gifts and talents of their children?
- Are parents provided with community resources to help them develop the talents of their children?
- Are parents provided with community resources to help them support the unique challenges the students may have in terms of learning or emotional needs?

Issue Four: Teachers and school personnel should be aware of the unique needs of these special populations of gifted students.

- Are there professional development opportunities where teachers and counselors learn about the needs of these students?

- Do teachers have resources both human and material to help them design and implement appropriate interventions?
- Do teachers have planning time to share ideas and develop strategies to meet the needs of these special youngsters?

Future Directions

As we enter the age of "No Child Left Behind" thinking, it would appear that the needs of these special populations of gifted students will be met. Unfortunately this is not the case. The methods sought under this federal policy are those scientifically proven to be effective to raise achievement of students. These strategies tend to be minimalistic and focus on basic skill acquisition rather than talent development. Furthermore, funds for talent development are always tenuous. The limited funds available are often allocated to provide services for more traditional groups of gifted students. Little funds, if any, are reserved for guidance and counseling except for students who are already in severe difficulty.

Currently many bright students from special populations are not identified as gifted because their unique characteristics prevent them from meeting traditional criteria. Some students who are diagnosed as having severe learning, behavioral, or attention problems are excluded from admission into a gifted program or from receiving talent development services. This may occur because professionals in special education are not always aware of the characteristic behaviors of gifted students or what happens when remediation is substituted for talent development (Baum & Olenchak, 2002). To worsen matters, procedures for identifying and accommodating gifted children with learning disabilities and other learning differences are changing. Students who are bright but achieve at grade level may fall through the cracks of being served at all.

Although this projection is bleak, it is a call to arms. It is imperative that we advocate for the needs of these students. Parents, educators, and professionals who care about these special populations need to unite and take a stand. They need to become politically active to draw attention to the unique needs of these students. Researchers need to conduct the experimental studies that can prove the efficacy of providing talent development and counseling services to these special students at risk.

REFERENCES

Baldwin, A. (1978). Curriculum and methods—What is the difference? In A. Y. Baldwin, G. H. Gear, & L. J. Lucito (Eds.), *Educational planning for the gifted: Overcoming cultural, geographic, and socioeconomic barriers* (pp. 37-49). Reston, VA: Council for Exceptional Children.

Baum, S. (1988). An enrichment program for gifted learning disabled students. *Gifted Child Quarterly. 32*(1), 226-230. **[See Vol. 7, p. 1.]**

xxxii   Twice-Exceptional and Special Populations of Gifted Students

Baum, S., Cooper, C., & Neu, T. (2001). Dual differentiation: An approach for meeting the curricular needs of gifted students with learning disabilities. *Psychology in the Schools, 38*, 477-490.

Baum, S., Olenchak, F. R., & Owen, S. Y., (1998). Gifted students with attention deficits: Fact and/or fiction? Or, can we see the forest for the trees?. *Gifted Child Quarterly. 42*(2), 96-104. **[See Vol. 7, p. 35.]**

Baum, S., & Olenchak, F. R. (2002). The alphabet children: GT, ADHD and more. *Exceptionality, 10*(2), 77-91.

Baum, S., & Owen, S. V. (in press). *Alphabet children: Gifted students with learning disabilities and more.* Mansfield Center, CT: Creative Learning Press.

Bernal, E. (2002). Three ways to achieve a more equitable representation of culturally and linguistically different students in GT programs. *Roeper Review, 24*(2), 82-88.

Chae, P. K., Kim, J. H., & Sun Noh, K. (2003). Diagnosis of ADHD among gifted children in relation to *KEDI-WISC* and *T.O.V.A.* performance. *Gifted Child Quarterly, 47*(3), 192-201.

P.L. 95-561, title IX, Part A. (1978). *The Jacob Javits gifted and talented children education act of 1978.*

Ford, D. Y., Harris, J. J., Tyson, C.A., & Trotman, M. F. (2002). Beyond deficit thinking: providing access for gifted African American students. *Roeper Review, 24*(2), 52-58.

Frasier, M. (1980). Programming for the culturally diverse. In J. B. Jordan, & J. A. Grossi (Eds.), *An introductory administrator's handbook on designing programs for the gifted and talented* (pp. 56-65). Reston, VA: Council for Exceptional Children.

Gardner, H. (1983). *Frames of Mind.* New York: Basic Books.

Grantham, T. C. (2002). Underrepresentation in Gifted Education: How Did We Get Here and What Needs to Change? Straight Talk on the Issue of Underrepresentation: An Interview with Dr. Mary M. Frasier, *Roeper Review, 24*(1), 50-51.

Maker, J. (1977). *Providing programs for the gifted handicapped.* Reston,VA: Council for Exceptional Children.

Neihart, M. (2000). Gifted children with Asperger's Syndrome. *Gifted Child Quarterly, 44*(4), 222-230. **[See Vol. 7, p. 51.]**

Oreck, B., Baum, S., & McCartney, H. (2000). *Artistic talent development for urban youth: The promise and the challenge.* (Research Monograph No. RM00144). Storrs: University of Connecticut, The National Research Center on the Gifted and Talented.

Peterson, J. S., & Rischar, H. (2000). Gifted and gay: A study of the adolescent experience. *Gifted Child Quarterly 44*(4), 231-246. **[See Vol. 7, p.**

Reis, S. M. (1987). We can't change what we can't recognize: Understanding the special needs of gifted females. *Gifted Child Quarterly, 31*(2), 83-89. **[See Vol. 7, p.**

Reis, S. M. (1998). *Work left undone.* Mansfield Center, CT: Creative Learning Press.

Reis, S. M., McGuire, J. M., & Neu, T. W. (2000). Compensation strategies used by high-ability students with learning disabilities who succeed in college. *Gifted Child Quarterly, 44*(2), 123-34. **[See Vol. 7, p. 13.]**

Renzulli, J. S. (1978). What makes giftedness: Reexamining a definition. *Phi DeltaKappan, 60*, 180-184.

Renzulli, J. S., & Park, S. (2000). Gifted dropouts: The who and the why. *Gifted Child Quarterly, 44*(4), 261-271. **[See Vol. 7, p. 117.]**

Sears, P. (1979). The Terman genetic studies of genius, 1922-1972. In A.H. Passow (Ed.) *The gifted and talented* (pp. 75-96). Chicago: National Society for the Study of Education.

Slocumb, P., & Payne, R. (2000). *Removing the mask: Giftedness in poverty.* Highlands, Texas: RFT Publishing.

Spicker, H. S., Southern, W. T., & Davis, B. I. (1987). The rural gifted child. *Gifted Child Quarterly, 31*(4), 155-157. **[See Vol. 7, p. 109.]**

Sternberg, R. (1986). Identifying the gifted through IQ: Why a little bit of knowledge is a dangerous thing. *Roeper Review, 8*(3), 143-147.

Terman, L. (1925). *Genetic studies of genius: Volume 1. Mental and physical traits of a thousand gifted children.* Stanford, CA: Stanford University Press.

Terman, L., & Oden, M. (1947). *Genetic studies of genius: Volume 4. The gifted child grows up.* Stanford, CA: Stanford University Press.

Tomlinson, C. A., Callahan, C. M., & Lelli, K. M. (1997). Challenging expectations: Case studies of high potential, culturally diverse young children. *Gifted Child Quarterly, 41*(1), pp. 5-18.

Whitmore, J. (1980). *Giftedness, conflict and underachievement.* Boston: Allyn & Bacon.

1

An Enrichment Program for Gifted Learning Disabled Students

Susan Baum

College of New Rochelle

Professionals interested in gifted/learning disabled students have found that these students have educational needs different from those of their learning disabled peers with average ability. This article describes and evaluates a pilot enrichment program designed to meet their needs. Seven bright learning disabled youngsters in grades 4 and 5 met for 2½ hours a week over a nine-month period to develop their strengths and interests through challenging enrichment activities. Six of the seven students showed gains in self-esteem, learning behavior, and creative productivity.

Editor's Note: From Baum, S. (1988). An enrichment program for gifted learning disabled students. *Gifted Child Quarterly*, 32(1), 226-230. © 1988 National Association for Gifted Children. Reprinted with permission.

Jimmy, a somewhat immature, task-avoiding 9-year-old, excitedly declared, "I'm going to sign my contract to conduct the research and start a campaign to get kids to wear bicycle helmets. I know it will be hard and some days I won't feel like working, but it's such an important project."

"I never thought I'd be able to create my own slide and tape show. Is it really going to be shown at the Noah Webster House?" Her eyes sparkled as Debra recounted her role as a director, writer, and actress in her historical research project, "A Day in the Life of Drusella Webster." Both youngsters were part of a program specifically designed to develop strengths and interests in gifted learning disabled students.

Traditionally, students who demonstrate a substantial discrepancy between performance and ability are diagnosed as learning disabled. Once identified, these students are provided with remediation in deficit areas with little or no attention given to strengths. In fact, the students diagnosed as learning disabled who also exhibit superior abilities are offered the same remedial menu as their average ability disabled peers. Is the menu equally suitable for the two groups? Or do gifted learning disabled students have unique characteristics which suggest alternate educational practices?

Gifted learning disabled students have been reported to be productive in non-academic settings (Baum, 1984; Schiff, Kaufman, & Kaufman, 1981; Whitmore, 1980). While their school performance is often poor, once outside the school environment these students seem to have hobbies and interests that require keen motivation and creative thinking. Schiff et al. (1981) document that "uneven gifted" students are often creative producers in the arts and sciences in their homes. Hokanson and Jospe (1976) also claim that in non-academic settings it is possible to observe in these students "rapid learning of high interest material, and an ability to construct and organize" (p. 32).

According to a recent study (Baum, 1985) comparing gifted, gifted/LD and average LD students, gifted/LD students were found to be more creative than their LD peers. In fact, they had more productive extra-curricular interests than both other groups. However, gifted/LD students were also found to be the most disruptive in school and perceived themselves as academic failures with a poor sense of academic self-efficacy, whereas both other groups were more satisfied with their school performance.

The fact that bright learning disabled students have a poorer sense of academic self-efficacy than their learning disabled peers when they possess greater intellectual and creative potential must be examined more closely. Self-efficacy, according to Bandura (1982), is the perception that a person can organize and carry out some action. These judgments in turn influence thoughts, behaviors, and emotional arousal. Because they tend to be situational, these perceptions influence choice of activity and environmental settings. Increased self-efficacy results from success experiences and reciprocally motivates better performance.

Remediation procedures are typically based on structured learning into manageable tasks to ensure success. Success, in turn, should improve feelings of self-efficacy, and thus increase future achievement. If LD/Average students do not perceive themselves as school failures, this approach seems effective for them. However, for gifted/LD this is probably not the case. Bandura (1982) asserts that self-efficacy is gained from those performance accomplishments that the individual respects and perceives as a challenge. Achievements are perceived as successes depending on how well the accomplishment meets the internal standards of the student. Mastery of simple, routine tasks may not be viewed as an accomplishment for gifted/LD students when they succeed in complex tasks at home. For example, mastering short 'a' is still not reading. In essence, there appears to be no acceptable outlet in school for meaningful and challenging productivity found outside of school—a situation that may explain misbehavior and a sense of failure in the school setting.

The results of this study of comparative behavior encouraged us to establish a special enrichment program for gifted/LD youngsters in which meaningful outlets would be provided. This program would be based on four assumptions. First, special enrichment activities designed to develop the students' superior talents are required if their potential is to be realized. Second, these activities must encompass both interests and strengths of the students as well as provide sophisticated challenges to motivate their bright minds. Third, the enrichment activities must be designed to circumvent problematic weaknesses and to highlight abstract thinking and creative production. Last, creative behavior of the students must be reinforced and appreciated within the school setting if it is to be maintained in a producive manner. The purpose of this article is to describe the program and discuss its results.

THE PILOT PROGRAM

Setting

Seven gifted learning disabled students met every Wednesday for two and one-half hours at the district's resource center for gifted students. The time selected for the program was an extension of a weekly shortened day used by the district for staff development purposes, thereby eliminating lost class time for students. A teacher and an intern, both specialists in gifted and special education, planned and implemented the program.

Identification

The identification process entailed screening the district's ninety-nine learning disabled students in grades four through six for characteristics of gifted behavior. In this district learning disabled students were those who performed below grade level and evidenced a significant discrepancy between ability and achievement as determined by a discrepancy formula. Gifted behavior was defined as the potential to develop "the dynamic interaction among three clusters of traits: well above average ability, creativity, and task commitment, that an individual brings to bear on a specific area of human endeavor" (Renzulli, 1978). Ideally, identification efforts for special programs should focus on locating a talent pool of bright students; program goals should emphasize the development of creativity and task commitment in these students (Renzulli and Reis, 1985). Because the resources of the model program did not permit working with a talent pool of bright learning disabled youngsters, the decision was made to select from such a pool those students who already demonstrated creativity and task commitment somewhere in their lives. These students would participate in advanced levels of enrichment in an effort to help them redirect and integrate individual but isolated traits into creative production.

Both test scores and teacher interviews were used to gain information about these students. Well above-average ability was identified by assessment of scores of the Wechsler Intelligence Scale for Children/Revised (Wechsler, 1974). Students scoring at least 120 on the performance or verbal scale were selected for further screening. Fourteen students met the initial criterion. To gain information about creativity and task commitment in these students, classroom teachers and learning disabilities teachers were interviewed with an adaptation of the Scales of Rating Behavioral Characteristics of Superior Students (Renzulli, Smith, White, Callahan & Hartman, 1976). The adapted questionnaire consisted of 20 open-ended items from the Learning, Creativity and Motivation subscales. For example, one item asked teachers to describe an instance when the student became totally absorbed in a particular topic. The resulting information was analyzed by a team consisting of a school psychologist, a special education coordinator, and a university researcher. Each student was given a score averaged across raters based on evidences of advanced and persistent interests, creativity behaviors, and specific personality traits often demonstrated by creative individuals. The students' final scores were derived by averaging the individual ratings. Selection for the pilot program was made by rank-ordering the fourteen students according to their average score and selecting the top seven. (Seven was determined to be an optimum number of students considering the hyperactive behavior and attention deficit problems commonly occurring in this population).

Of the seven students identified, 5 were boys and 2 girls; four were fourth graders and 3 were fifth graders. Full scale IQ, Verbal IQ, and Performance IQ scores ranged from 134–113; 139–107; and 132–112 respectively. All students had clearly defined interests and preferred projects and experiments to written and reading assignments. Their creativity was evidenced in the clever ways they avoided tasks, their sense of humor, ideas, and completed projects in science, art, and storytelling (as opposed to story writing.)

The Program

The Enrichment Triad Model (Renzulli, 1977) was chosen for this program. This model incorporates skill development into the production of new knowledge through the pursuit of independent or small group investigations based on the student's own interests and academic strengths. Children are encouraged to identify an area of interest and then focus on a real problem to be investigated and possibly solved. The model consists of three types of activities: general exploratory; group training; and individual and small group investigation.

General exploratory activities cover exposure to potential areas of interest not necessarily found in the regular curriculum. For learning disabled students, these areas may be introduced through lectures, demonstrations, movies, interest centers, or other approaches that bypass weaknesses in reading. These no-fail entry activities expose students to new ideas in a nonthreatening atmosphere where they are given the opportunity to explore freely.

The next step—Type II enrichment activities—provide training in such areas as critical thinking, creativity, and problem solving. Because learning disabled children often perform better on activities using higher-level thinking skills as opposed to simple memory and perceptual capacities (Maker, 1977), these types of activities are quite appropriate.

In Type III activities the student becomes an investigator of a real problem—one that has not been contrived as a classroom assignment—and is guided in the development of a product that should have an authentic impact on an audience, preferably outside the school setting. The student focuses on an original idea for study and proceeds as a "practicing professional" using methods of inquiry to solve a chosen problem.

During weekly sessions, Type I and Type II experiences were provided. They were designed to spark the children's interests in a future investigation and to broaden their means of effective communication to compensate for poor reading and writing skills. Specific activities included exposure to, and instruction in, photography, computer programming, and block construction.

To expose the students to the process of creative production, a student-initiated group project was undertaken. The students wrote and illustrated a unique children's book on unusual ways to pop a balloon. They designed and photographed scenes to express their ideas and wrote rhymed couplets to accompany their illustrations. To avoid using their poor handwriting, the students elected to use presstype letters, which, although tedious, was more effective in creating a professional-looking product. This project gave the students experience in staying on a task, solving problems, using new communication skills and delaying gratification.

Upon completion of the book, the students were encouraged to initiate individual investigations. Conferences were held with each student to assist in identifying a real problem, defining a purpose and a concerned audience for the study, and selecting a final product. A step-by step management plan and a contract with clear expectations were developed for each student to facilitate product completion. Two students designed computer programs. One program taught fifth graders about the *Monitor* and *Merrimac*; the other used random numbers to define traits of Dungeons and Dragons characters. A 9-year-old girl with limited reading and writing ability conducted a qualitative research study entitled "A Day in the Life of Drusella Webster" (Noah Webster's younger sister) and produced a slide and tape show which is on permanent display in the Noah Webster House. Another student compared attitudes of adults and children about wearing bicycle helmets. He communicated his results on an attractive poster designed for display in bicycle shops to encourage the wearing of helmets. Another young researcher prepared a dramatic slide-tape show of fifth graders' attitudes concerning nuclear war and sent it to her state senator. Another investigation sought to create an awareness of the plight of endangered species, while another student decided to use Lego bricks to create models of castles and give a series of talks about the use of castles during the Middle Ages.

Students met with expert professionals to help them in development of their research products. A university professor in measurement and evaluation taught several of the students to construct surveys and sample a population. Museum curators met with the students investigating historical and environmental issues. Consultants from the Lego Corporation offered advice to the young architect. A mentor in computers assisted the other two students in creating their computer programs. All but one project was completed and shared with the intended audience. Time needed to complete their projects ranged from 4–10 weeks.

Results

The success of the program was assessed according to the extent that the program objectives specified below were realized. A discussion of each objective follows:

Objective #1. Students will successfully complete an individual creative product. Six of seven children completed products. The products were assessed using the Student Product Assessment Form (Renzulli & Reis, 1981) by experienced teachers of the gifted who had no knowledge of this pilot program or that the students were learning disabled. This instrument was designed to evaluate the quality of projects of students in gifted programs and provides individual ratings for eight specific qualitative characteristics of student products as well as seven factors related to overall product quality. Each characteristic is followed by an item description and examples of student's work that illustrates the concept being rated. A 5-point scale ranging from 1 to 5 was used to evaluate the eight characteristics. The average ratings for the individual projects are shown in Table 1. A rating between 4 and 5 connotes an excellent product (Reis, 1984).

As evidenced by the ratings reported in Table 1, five out of the seven students completed products comparable to high quality products of gifted non-disabled students.

An outside evaluator was contracted to assess objectives two and three. Observation of children, questionnaires and interviews of parents and teachers were used to gain information.

Table 1   Project Rating on the Student Product Assessment Form

Student	Project	Average Rating
1	Nuclear War	4.1
2	Dungeons and Dragon Program	4.0
3	Castle	Not Completed
4	*Merrimac* and *Monitor* Program	4.0
5	Bicycle Survey	4.2
6	Historical Research	4.42
7	Poster on Endangered Species	2.8

Objective #2. Student learning behavior will show improvement as demonstrated by increased time on task and sustained effort toward task completion. At the onset of the program, the students' observed rate of effort on most independent tasks ranged from ten to twenty minutes. Often the students complained when asked to put forth any effort at all. Typical comments included, "Do we have to do this? I thought this program was supposed to be fun."

Observations during the group project indicated an increase in individual student's time on task and level of enthusiasm. Students could sustain effort for as long as an hour depending on the nature of the task. Even when frustrated, students would ask to be excused from a given task but volunteered to complete another task equally as important and time consuming, but easier for that student. One student who had poor motor coordination had a difficult time using presstype. Totally frustrated with that task, he offered to go to the library to survey children's books for possible publishers and record their names and addresses. It took him one hour to complete the project which he accomplished independently. The students remained interested in working on the book during the eight weeks needed for its completion.

When students were involved in their own independent research, time on task increased dramatically. Students were observed to be on task up to 2½ hours during some class periods collecting and analyzing data and arranging their presentations. Several students voluntarily worked on their projects at home. The parent of one child reported that the child had worked 3½ hours to perfect her final project. The duration of time needed to complete the individual projects ranged from four to ten weeks.

Objective #3. Students will show improvement in self-esteem. Improvement in self-esteem was documented by teacher and parent interviews. Except for the one student who did not complete the product, this improvement was noted in all the children. Sample comments from parent and regular classroom teacher interviews include the following:

- Our son finally feels that he has the ability to achieve.
- The students in my classroom have new respect for the child since she shared her excellent project.

- She is so much more independent now. She acts like a different child in your room. She has come alive.
- He is attempting to do many new things this year. He even had the courage to run for class president.
- He has so many interests, but never followed through on any. He's so proud of his accomplishment.

Objective #4. Strategies will be developed to implement the Enrichment Triad Model for the gifted learning disabled students. The process of working with gifted learning disabled students was developed. Specific teaching strategies that provided the structure so vital to the children's success were implemented as we worked with the children. The strategies fell into 3 categories: (1) selecting appropriate activities, (2) managing behavior, and (3) helping students compensate for weaknesses. Specific examples of these strategies are listed below.

Selecting appropriate activities.

1. Use active inquiry involving discussion and experimentation.

2. Provide open-ended challenges requiring divergent thinking especially in small group settings.

3. Consider students' preferred learning styles, interests, and strengths.

4. Incorporate opportunities for students to investigate real problems for real audiences based on student interest.

5. Provide sufficient time for involved students to work without interruption.

Managing behavior.

1. Encourage the students to assume responsibilities.

2. To enhance motivation pair activities so that the less desirable task precedes a preferred task.

3. Limit choices. Too many choices interfere with decision-making.

4. Provide clear information about student expectations. Contracts are helpful in getting the student to understand steps involved.

5. Use environmental settings as cues for desired behavior. Private offices can be created for independent work. Sit students around a small table for informal group discussions as they often need the structure that the table supplies. When changing activities, change the setting.

Helping students compensate for weaknesses.

1. Pair students whose strengths are complementary—a reader with a writer.

2. Find sources of information that are appropriate for students—picture books, tapes or lectures for non-readers; word processors for non-writers.

3. Make the students aware of individual strengths and weaknesses. Encourage them to choose tasks that rely on strengths rather than magnify weaknesses.

4. Be sensitive to students' frustration levels. Provide an appropriate escape route where s/he can drop out with integrity.

Summary and Conclusions

The pilot program for gifted learning disabled students demonstrated the short-term positive effects of providing an enrichment program based on the Enrichment Triad Model. Learning behaviors, time on task, and motivation showed marked improvement when the students selected their own interest area, became personally involved with their product, and were directed toward a goal.

Students' projects all reflected their individual learning styles, interests, and strengths. They gained information through primary sources such as interviews, visitations, surveys, and evaluation of actual artifacts. Students chose to communicate their ideas through slide shows, computer programs, surveys, and charts. An unexpected result was reported by parents and teachers. Academic achievement in four out of the seven children improved dramatically. One student will no longer need supportive services; another gained four grade levels in reading during the year; two others have begun to show improvements in all subject areas.

Educational Implications

The findings of this study offer important guidelines to professionals who work with gifted learning disabled students in regular classrooms and special settings. These guidelines are discussed below with specific examples of how the guidelines may be implemented.

Focused attention should be given to the development of a gift or talent in its own right. Perhaps the major reason this program was successful was that, for the first time, these students were singled out for their special abilities rather than their disability. The program enriched rather than remediated.

Gifted learning disabled students require a supportive environment which values and appreciates individual abilities. In the enrichment program students were encouraged to gain information and communicate their ideas in creative ways based on their individual strengths. Guest speakers, demonstrations, active inquiry, visitations, and films were used to help the students gain information in lieu of reading and listening to "teacher talk." The students' products, in turn, took the form of slides, models, speeches, computer programs, drama, and film rather than written reports. Thus, their disability was minimized while their strengths were highlighted.

Students should be given strategies to compensate for their learning problems as well as direct instruction in basic skills. The students in the model program were allowed to circumvent weaknesses to accomplish their goals. Students who had difficulty with writing and spelling were taught to use the word processor and spelling programs. Photography allowed products to be impressive and effective. Technology has provided efficient means to organize and access information, increase accuracy in mathematics and spelling, and enhance the quality of communication, the areas that gifted/LD students find difficult. These students should be allowed to "author" without getting bogged down with the physical act of "writing" or solve abstract problems in math without agonizing over math facts never permanently mastered.

Last, but perhaps most important, *gifted learning disabled students must become aware of their strengths and weaknesses and be helped to cope with the wide discrepancy between them.* The students in the model program were told that the enrichment program was designed to focus on their special abilities whereas their learning disabilities program would continue to provide remedial support.

Gifted/LD students should continue to receive assistance in areas of weakness; however, special time must be purposefully set aside to help these students recognize and develop their gifts as well as understand the motivational and affective requirements necessary for achieving success. Participation in established programs for gifted students or specially designed programs for gifted/LD students like the one described here will provide such support.

REFERENCES

Bandura, A. (1982). Self-efficacy mechanism in human agency. *American Psychologist, 37,* 122–147.

Baum, S. (1984). Meeting the needs of learning disabled gifted students. *Roeper Review, 7,* 16–19.

Baum, S. (1985). *Learning disabled students with superior cognitive abilities: A validation study of descriptive behaviors.* Unpublished doctoral dissertation, University of Connecticut.

Hoakanson, D. T., & Jospe, M. (1976). *The search for cognitive giftedness in exceptional children.* Hartford, CT: Connecticut State Department of Education.

Maker, C. J. (1977). *Providing programs for gifted handicapped.* Reston, VA: Council for Exceptional Children.

Reis, S. (1984). Personal communication, July, 19.

Renzulli, J. S. (1977). *The enrichment triad model: A guide for developing defensible programs for the gifted and talented.* Mansfield Center, CT: Creative Learning Press.

Renzulli, J. S. (1978). What makes giftedness? Reexamining a definition. *Phi Delta Kappan, 60,* 180–184.

Renzulli, J. S., & Reis, S. M. (1981). *Student product assessment form.* In J. Renzulli, S. Reis, and L. Smith, *Revolving door identification model.* Mansfield Center, CT: Creative Learning Press.

Renzulli, J. S., & Reis, S. (1985). *The schoolwide enrichment model: A comprehensive plan for educational excellence.* Mansfield Center, CT: Creative Learning Press.

Renzulli, J. S., Smith, L. H., White, A. J., Callahan, C. M., & Hartman, R. K. (1976). Scales for rating the behavioral characteristics of superior students. Mansfield Center, CT.: Creative Learning Press.

Schiff, M., Kaufman, N., & Kaufman, A. (1981). Scatter analysis of WISC-R profiles for LD children with superior intelligence. *Journal of Learning Disabilities, 14,* 400–404.

Wechsler, D. (1974). *Wechsler intelligence scale for children, revised.* New York: Psychological Corporation.

Whitmore, J. R. (1980). *Giftedness, conflict and underachievement.* Boston: Allyn and Bacon.

2

Compensation Strategies Used by High-Ability Students With Learning Disabilities Who Succeed in College

Sally M. Reis

Joan M. McGuire

University of Connecticut

Terry W. Neu

Sacred Heart University

To investigate how high-ability students with learning disabilities succeed in postsecondary academic environments, 12 young adults with disabilities who were successful at the university level were studied. Extensive

Editor's Note: From Reis, S. M., McGuire, J. M., & Neu, T. W. (2000). Compensation strategies used by high-ability students with learning disabilities who succeed in college. *Gifted Child Quarterly, 44*(2), 123-134. © 2000 National Association for Gifted Children. Reprinted with permission.

interviews with these young adults provided examples of the problems faced by high-ability students with learning disabilities, as well as the specific compensation strategies they used to address and overcome these problems. Four of the participants had been identified as having a learning disability in elementary school; six were identified in junior or senior school; and two were not diagnosed until college. The participants believed that having a learning disability was considered by elementary or secondary school personnel as synonymous with below-average ability. They reported that content remediation, rather than instruction compensatory strategies, was usually provided in elementary and secondary school learning disability programs. In this article, the compensation strategies used by academically gifted students who succeeded in college are discussed. These include: study strategies, cognitive/learning strategies, compensatory supports, environmental accommodations, opportunities for counseling, self-advocacy, and the development of an individual plan incorporating a focus on metacognition and executive functions.

Although researchers have reported that gifted students with learning disabilities are often productive in nonacademic settings (Baum, 1984; Brody & Mills, 1997; Fox, Brody, & Tobin, 1983; Reis, Neu, & McGuire, 1995; Schiff, Kaufman, & Kaufman, 1981; Whitmore, 1980), limited research has been conducted on how these high-ability students with learning disabilities succeed in school. Even less research exists among college students with learning disabilities who also exhibit attributes associated with giftedness. Given the recent trend of increasing numbers of students with learning disabilities enrolling in postsecondary settings (Henderson, 1995), it is likely that high-ability students who also experience learning disabilities are represented among this population. Without information that sheds light on the variables affecting the success of these students in postsecondary academic settings, both secondary and postsecondary personnel are left to speculate about interventions that will facilitate effective transition to an environment characterized by vastly different demands.

Putting the Research to Use

Many high-ability students with learning disabilities experience both frustration and difficulty in school as they get older and the content of their classes becomes increasingly difficult. Many are never identified because their learning disability masks their giftedness and their giftedness masks their learning disability. Current learning disability programs may not provide the special skills necessary to succeed in school for those who are identified. The research reported in this study details the compensation strategies used by successful university students with learning disabilities. Many of these students learned how to be academically successful when they participated in a university program for students with learning disabilities and had the opportunity to learn specific compensation strategies.

Too few learning disability programs focus on teaching compensation strategies for students with learning disabilities, and it would appear that only a minute number of districts offer any specialized training in these strategies for gifted students with learning disabilities. Instead of teaching compensation strategies, most of these programs appear to focus on students' immediate curriculum needs, such as content remediation and help with specific content and homework. Many of the participants in this study believed that if they had learned the compensation strategies described in this article when they were in elementary or secondary school, they would have been much more successful students, especially in secondary school. Both special educators and gifted educators should reexamine learning disability programs currently in place in many schools. High-ability students with learning disabilities will benefit from acquiring the specific compensation strategies described in this article. Indeed, these compensation strategies seem to be essential to both the academic and personal success of this population.

In one of only a few studies examining school-age high-ability students with learning disabilities, Baum and Owen (1988) found them to possess unique characteristics related to both persistence and individual interests. They also noted lower academic self-efficacy among their sample in comparison with peers without giftedness and learning disabilities. According to Bandura (1986), self-efficacy is the self-perception that a person can organize and carry out some action. Studies reveal that it is the beliefs an individual holds regarding his or her personal efficacy that shape academic performance, as well as career choices (Bandura, 1997). If some high-ability students with learning disabilities perceive themselves as less able to achieve in academic tasks, identification of the strategies used by successful high-ability students with learning disabilities could contribute to interventions that help students learn how to deal with the "paradox of the average student who is not the average thinker" (Vail, 1989, p. 136).

Other researchers (Shore & Dover, 1987; Sternberg, 1981) have found that the use of metacognition, defined by Flavell, Miller, and Miller (1993) as "cognition about cognition" (p. 150), and problem-solving skills to process information faster and more effectively is associated with gifted students. In several case studies of gifted students with learning disabilities (Baum, Owen, & Dixon, 1991; Daniels, 1983; Vail, 1987; Whitmore & Maker, 1985), the frustration between understanding complex information and having a disability in information processing emerges as a factor with implications for student self-efficacy, as well as interventions. The demands of college, including autonomy, self-monitoring, and problem solving, require students to adjust to multiple setting and task demands, and the development of strategies to enhance these skills may be particularly appropriate for high-ability students with learning disabilities (Miller, Rzonca, & Snider, 1991).

The work of Gerber and Reiff (1991) and Gerber, Ginsberg, and Reiff (1992) has contributed powerful observations from highly successful adults with learning disabilities with respect to strategies they view as integral to vocational success and adult adjustment. These highly successful adults emphasize their potential to achieve rather than stressing the deficits of the disability. Factors such as persistence, self-confidence, the will to conquer adversity, and strong character have been cited as contributing to the success of individuals with disabilities (Maker, 1978). Several themes emerged that increased the likelihood for vocational success, and the authors synthesized these patterns into one overriding factor: the desire and effort to gain control of one's life. A greater degree of that control indicated more likelihood of succeeding in life. Factors that emerged from extensive interviews with these adults from 24 states and Canada included control or taking charge of their lives; the desire to succeed; goal-orientation; reframing or reinterpreting the disability in a positive sense; persistence; goodness of fit between strengths, weaknesses, and career choice; learned creativity or divergent thinking; and a social ecology of support systems, including family and friends. Remediation of their learning disability was not a major factor in the lives of these successful adults.

Remediation of basic skills deficits through repetition to ensure mastery has proven ineffective for high-ability students with learning disabilities (Baum, 1984; Baum & Owen, 1988; Daniels, 1986; Jacobson, 1984; Whitmore, 1980). Educators must examine the underlying rationale of the interventions provided for these students, especially as they progress into secondary settings where compensatory approaches may better prepare students for the demands of higher education. The development of coping or compensatory strategies to perform a task in a different manner (e.g., using an audiotape to accompany text material) has, in fact, been cited as a major benefit by college graduates with learning disabilities (Adelman & Vogel, 1993).

COMPENSATION STRATEGIES

Crux (1991) defined compensation strategies to include study strategies, cognitive strategies (also called learning strategies), compensatory supports (e.g., tape recorders and computer word processing programs), and environmental accommodations such as test-taking accommodations (e.g., extended test time, less distracting test-taking setting). Other researchers (Garner, 1988; Mayer, 1988) have noted that learning strategies comprise behaviors of a learner that are intended to enhance information processing. Rather than focusing on what is to be learned (i.e., the content), instruction in cognitive strategies emphasizes learning how to learn. Specific learning strategies (e.g., repetition, verbal elaboration, organization techniques, paraphrasing, association) gradually come under the control of efficient learners through executive function processes or self-regulation. Competent learners are proficient in their capacity to choose strategies according to the demands of a task, monitor strategy usage, and adapt or devise strategic behavior using a problem-solving paradigm (Borkowski & Burke, 1996). Very little has been written about compensation strategies for gifted students with learning disabilities in elementary and secondary schools. Baum et al. (1991) suggested that high-ability students with learning disabilities should be able to work within their interest areas while also addressing their disabilities. Since so few compensation strategies are suggested for elementary or secondary students, an excellent explanation of the use of specific compensation strategy service delivery systems can be found in the education of university students with learning disabilities (Adelman & Vogel, 1993; Brinckerhoff, Shaw, & McGuire, 1993; Shaw, Brinckerhoff, Kistler, & McGuire, 1992).

Study and Performance and Counseling Strategies

As noted by Crux (1991), study strategies comprise a component of the compensation strategies that are very important for these adult learners. In a comprehensive study of learning specialists' logs that recorded the activities of sessions with university students with learning disabilities, McGuire, Hall, and Litt (1991) found specific areas commonly addressed in a successful university program for students with learning disabilities. These included study strategies, course-related performance strategies (e.g., reading comprehension and written expression), counseling, and self-advocacy training. Study strategies and specific skills to compensate for the learning disability emerged as the overwhelming need of university students with learning disabilities, including specific types of note-taking strategies, time management, test-taking preparation, and library skills. Note-taking strategies are not typically taught in the regular university curriculum, yet are critical for the organization of information delivered in classes.

Time management was the most frequently occurring objective among study strategies. The use of one-month organizers and semester overview calendars was consistently modeled and further enhanced by analyzing each week, and sometimes each day, to maximize the students' use of time. Time management has been found to depend on students' abilities to self-monitor their activities and make appropriate decisions based upon awareness of the extra time required to complete academic tasks in the area of the specific disability.

The actual instruction of test-taking skills is rarely provided in students' educational experience (Bragstad & Stumpf, 1987). For successful university students with learning disabilities, learning specialists usually facilitated a plan for test preparation, modeled strategies for analyzing multiple choice questions, suggested methods to reduce test-taking anxiety, and trained students to use an error analysis approach to review tests and pinpoint reasons for incorrect answers (McGuire et al., 1991).

Strategies related to classroom performance, such as written expression, reading comprehension, and mathematical processes, were also modeled and facilitated by learning specialists (McGuire et al., 1991). Written expression instruction helped students in the development of skills such as the organization of written assignments, proofreading, and sentence structure and mechanics. Learning specialists also addressed the need for compensatory strategies using word processing and other software packages for some individuals. To aid students with reading comprehension, learning specialists provided modeling and practice in paraphrasing, highlighting the text, identifying main ideas and supporting details, and training in a technique known as SQ3R (Survey, Question, Read, Recite, Review). This strategy provides a reading format that promotes an organized approach to absorb written information (Bragstad & Stumpf, 1987). Content materials from a course the student was taking were used to provide the opportunity to apply strategies and reinforce transfer (McGuire et al., 1991).

Counseling for university students with learning disabilities comprised one-third of the learning specialists' instructional time (McGuire et al., 1991) and included academic, personal, and career concerns. For example, students were encouraged to consider balancing their academic courseload in light of their learning strengths and weaknesses. If rate of reading was a problem, students were advised to adjust their selection of courses to avoid a class schedule that required a great deal of reading. Students were also advised of the other more clinical counseling services available to them at the university.

SELF-ADVOCACY

High-ability students with learning disabilities often need guidance in understanding their strengths and weaknesses in order to utilize appropriate strategies and advocate for academic accommodations. Self-advocacy involves the recognition of these strengths and weaknesses and the students' skills in presenting their abilities, as well as weaknesses, in their communication with faculty. This self-awareness enables students to request accommodations such as extra time on tests, alternative testing environments, or extensions for assignments. Again, self-monitoring is essential.

EXECUTIVE FUNCTIONS AND METACOGNITION

Executive functions and metacognition contribute to compensation strategies for high-ability students. Executive functions were defined by Stuss and Benson (1986) as the planning and sequencing of complex behaviors, the ability to pay attention to several components at once, the capacity for grasping the gist of a complex situation, the resistance to distraction and interference, the inhibition of inappropriate response tendencies, and the ability to sustain behavioral output for relatively prolonged periods. (p. 158)

Metacognition includes one's self-knowledge and self-regulation. Denckla (1989) proposed that school-related behaviors within the executive function domain include the abilities of proactive organization to initiate, shift, inhibit, and sustain; to plan, organize, and develop strategies or rules. These abilities, or lack thereof, according to Denckla, make a significant contribution to the demonstration of learning disabilities.

Research has suggested that the improvement of learning ability includes the use of metacognition and executive function (Denckla, 1989; McGuire et al., 1991; Miller et al., 1991; Sternberg & Davidson, 1986). Because skilled learners and students with learning disabilities differ in metacognitive behaviors (Graham & Harris, 1987; Wong, 1987), interventions that train students to think about their thinking and engage in self-reflection and questioning are particularly important for success in postsecondary settings.

RESEARCH METHODS

The primary purpose of this study was to explore the perceptions of high-ability university students with learning disabilities regarding a variety of issues germane to their academic experiences (see Reis et al., 1995). This article addresses one facet of the broader study: the insights relating to compensation strategies used by gifted college students with learning disabilities to address their disabilities and result in successful academic performance. Qualitative methods were used in this study to investigate participants' perceptions about compensation strategies related to overcoming their learning disabilities. In order to obtain the most accurate image of the subjects' experiences and perceptions, open-ended questionnaires and in-depth interviews were used to explore both the participants' and their parents' perspectives and experiences. A questionnaire was used for demographic information and as a guide for extensive follow-up interview questions focusing on elementary and secondary school and university academic and social experiences.

Sample

Twelve university students with learning disabilities comprised the sample for this research (see Table 1). Experts in the University Program for College Students with Learning Disabilities initially selected participants from a pool of 140 university students with learning disabilities. Criteria for selection included: a) current university enrollment or graduation from the university during the year preceding the study; (b) identification as having a learning disability as verified by documentation required to establish eligibility for university services (McGuire, Shaw, & Anderson, 1992); (c) qualifications for designation as gifted on the basis of scores for IQ, achievement, and other indicators of performance (e.g., a notable talent in an area such as visual arts); and (d) academic success in the university setting. These individuals were identified as having a well-above-average or superior IQ in either elementary or secondary school (range 125–158), but had generally not been identified as gifted, usually because of lower achievement due to their learning disability. IQ scores on the Wechsler Adult Intelligence Scale Revised (WAIS-R) are included in Table 1, but it should be noted that IQ scores of several of the participants in this study declined from elementary to secondary school to college. Information used to document the label of giftedness in the selection for this study, in addition to IQ, included achievement tests results, academic awards, grades, outstanding performance in one or more academic areas, teacher nomination, elementary and secondary school records, and product information from an extensive academic portfolio. Approximately 20 students were initially identified for participation in this study, and their records were carefully screened. Letters of invitation were sent to 18 students, and the final selection of 12 took place based on interest and time available to participate in the study.

Data Collection

Gathering multiple viewpoints on a phenomenon, or triangulation, enables greater accuracy of interpretation than any of the data sources considered individually (Guba, 1978; Jick, 1983; Van Maanan, 1983). To ensure the highest degree of accuracy possible, data for this study were collected using three methods: document review of extensive records and testing information, written responses to an open-ended questionnaire, and in-depth interviews with each participant and one of his or her parents.

The open-ended questionnaire served as a preliminary source of issues investigated later during the interviews, which were conducted by two of the researchers. Before the initial interview, each participant and his or her parent were given written information about the study and his or her anticipated role in it. Each interview session was used to clarify, verify, and expand upon the participant's responses. All interviews were tape-recorded and transcribed, and the field notes and observations made by the researchers at the time of the interviews were added to the transcriptions. Interviews and other data collection procedures followed guidelines suggested by Spradley (1979), Strauss (1987), and Strauss and Corbin (1990). Participant and parent interviews were conducted by two of the researchers. The number of interviews conducted was determined when data saturation was reached; that is, when the participant could only provide information that was redundant and did not offer useful reinforcement of previously collected information (Spradley, 1979).

Table 1   Summary of Respondent Self-Report Questionnaire Data and WAIS-R Scores

Participant	Nature of the LD	Time period in which identified as LD	Time period in which identified as gifted	WAIS-R Scores		
				Verbal	Performance	Full Scale
Arthur	reading disability, slow processing of information	College	No	128	118	126
Colin	spelling, handwriting, poor short-term memory, reading, decoding	7th grade	7th grade	132	139	139
Diane	dyslexia, language problems	College	No	101	118	109
Evan	spelling, abstract math problems	11th grade	No	136	106	124
Fred	math, spelling, social problems	8th grade	No	120	126	126
Forrest	dyslexia, processing	7th grade	No	120	139	133
Jake	dyslexia, motor skills	6th grade	No	117	124	121
Joe	verbal and written expression, auditory	3rd grade	6th grade	142	132	140
Kate	language, spelling, reading	2nd grade	No	103	143	123
Mike	processing, attention deficit disorder	10th grade	No	106	122	133
Martin	dyslexia	1st grade	No	107	129	118
Peggy	slow thought process, spelling, penmanship, reading comprehension	5th grade	No	133	104	121

Data Analysis

Data analysis was conducted using techniques designed by Strauss (1987) and Strauss and Corbin (1990). As suggested by these researchers, data analysis coincided with data collection and affected the collection of additional data. Data analysis techniques included the use of a coding paradigm described by Strauss and Strauss and Corbin, as well as coding suggested by the same researchers, including three levels: open coding, axial coding, and selective coding.

The initial type of coding, known as open coding, involved unrestricted coding of all data included in field notes, interviews, and other pertinent documents. In open coding, data were analyzed and coded. As the researchers verified codes and determined relationships among and between codes, a determination was made about the relationship of a code to a category. After initial categories were determined, axial coding enabled the researchers to specify relationships among the many categories that emerged in open coding and, ultimately, resulted in the conceptualization of one or more categories selected as the "core." A core category accounted for most of the variation in a pattern of behavior; therefore, "the generation of theory occurs around a core category" (Strauss, 1987, p. 34). In the final stage of coding, selective coding, the relationships among categories were examined to determine the saturation of categories in the identification of the core category.

RESULTS

The early educational experiences of these students strongly influenced their approaches to compensating for their learning disabilities (Reis et al., 1995). During the interviews, all of the participants recalled negative and, in many cases painful, memories of elementary and secondary school experiences in which teachers accused them of being lazy because of the intersection of their abilities and disabilities. The learning disability programs in which some participated varied in organization and quality, and most students were critical of these programs. The reasons for the fluctuations in the quality of the special education learning disability program were numerous, including different teachers each year, no clear program goals, and a lack of a coherent program. Almost all of the respondents described scattered activities in an unclear, disorganized learning disability program. It should be noted that some of these students participated in new programs for students with learning disabilities. In some cases, students were placed in a program with many students whom they perceived to have more serious learning problems than they did. Many of the participants had a difficult time describing what they did in their elementary or high school learning disability program. Kate described her program as follows:

> I was, I guess, mainstreamed. I was put in a regular classroom with "normal students," and they would take me out for an hour every day or something, and I would go to a learning specialist or resource teacher, and then go over and do games and stuff like that.

Jake reflected on his public school program for students with learning disabilities:

> No, they hadn't gotten that far. Now that I think about it, they were kind of pretty backwards. We just worked on, like vocabulary and spelling. I

figured I guess they would teach you to spell better, then your disability would go away maybe.

These programs and the participants' negative elementary and secondary school experiences in general were not usually conducive to gaining compensation strategies or effective learning strategies. Not surprisingly, after the participants became involved in a university LD program, they reflected on how helpful it would have been if they had learned certain coping skills or strategies earlier. Martin explained,

I will complain to this day about high school and how they don't teach study skills. . . . This is the first time in my freshman year [at the university] that I had to use SQ3R as some kind of method of study. They never demanded it in my high school. In homework, I had maybe a little bit more than an hour, unless I had an exam.

Another participant concurred, explaining, "Yeah, I didn't realize then, so I do realize as I look back on it . . . just that they didn't demand you to use study skills."

Compensation Strategies

Multiple compensation strategies were employed by all of the participants in this study in order to succeed in challenging university settings, as indicated in Table 2. Each participant reported using all of the categories of compensation strategies listed in Table 2; however, the use of individual strategies within each category varied by participant. All participants attributed their success in their scholastic environments to their ability to employ these varied strategies. Study and time management strategies included, but were not limited to, methods of learning to study; note taking; identifying key points when reading and preparing for tests; library skills; and the use of daily, weekly, and monthly calendars. Among the compensation supports (Crux, 1991) reported were the use of computers, word processors, and books on tape. Executive functions included planning techniques, such as time management, metacognition, setting work priorities, and self-directed speech to help in difficult academic situations. Most of the participants in this study had previously learned some, but not many, compensation strategies without the benefit of a formal, structured learning disability program in their elementary or secondary careers. Peggy explained,

I learned to compensate for some of my learning problems, but for others, I was still working it out. I knew I had learning disabilities. I knew that was why I couldn't do things the same way other people did them, but I didn't necessarily know how to work it out [the other problems].

Diane, who did not fully understand the nature of her learning difficulties and how to compensate for them until she entered college, explained one of the compensation strategies she used to identify the best topics for her research papers. She would make appointments with her professors.

> Professors like to talk, and if I had to do a paper and couldn't find a topic, I would ask my professor what are the major research areas in the field. Then, I would go to the next professor and say, "What are top areas [in the same field]?" And I would go to each of the five professors in the field, ask the same questions, look at the lists they gave me, and identify the areas that matched.

Diane also cultivated friendships with persons in her classes whom she would invite to lunch. During lunch and after explaining about her learning disability, she would bring up the current work being done in class and turn the conversation toward the reading required for class, notes she had missed, or lectures that she hadn't understood. It was difficult, if not impossible, for many of the participants to listen and take notes at the same time. Mike and others used a similar compensation strategy. Mike, who had difficulty taking notes, explained what happened:

> I started to write things and stopped when I got lost and thought, "What am I going to do?" Luckily, a kid in my dorm was in my class, and I looked at his notes and I said, "Wow, this kid's got all the things I don't have." And it worked to my advantage. I used his notes and I started asking people if I could photocopy [their notes]. Up to date, I've always had at least one friend in the class. Every one of the classes that I've taken. It helps to be in a fraternity because you meet a lot of people, and you have a lot of brothers who have taken classes already or been in class with you.

By photocopying someone else's notes and comparing them with their own notes, participants in this study could determine whether they missed anything important during lectures.

Several of the students indicated that another compensation strategy they used was taking a reduced load of courses. Students who used this strategy usually took four or, occasionally, three classes a semester, as compared to five classes, which is normally considered a full course load at their university. This strategy provided the flexibility that is important if students must invest additional time and effort in their studying to compensate for disabilities.

Most of the students also used many of the compensation strategies available to them because of their identification as having a learning disability and their participation in UPLD (University Program for College Students with Learning Disabilities) (Brinckerhoff et al., 1993), such as extended time for examinations or taking an exam using a computer. Many requested extra help from professors who knew that these students had learning problems because they had disclosed their difficulties when requesting accommodations. Kate explained,

Table 2   Compensation Strategies Used by Gifted Students with Learning
Disabilities to Succeed

Strategy	Components
Study and Performance Strategies	Note taking
	Test-taking preparation
	Time management
	Monitoring daily, weekly, and monthly assignments and activities
	Using weekly and monthly organizers to maximize use of time; chunking assignments into workable parts
	Library skills
	Written expression
	Reading
	Mathematical processing
Cognitive/Learning Strategies	Memory strategies such as mnemonics and rehearsal using flash cards
	Chunking information into smaller units for mastery
Compensation Supports	Word processing
	Use of computers
	Books on tape

I work with my professors. I even go to one of my professors with my notebook, and she has time enough to sit with me and read through my notebook. She sees that I miss certain things, and she fills in my notebook. She fills in notes that I have missed. Another professor, I always go to him and just talk to him, and he goes through the stories with me, and I write everything, I am visual, so I write everything out and make little, not pictures, but sort of like trees and attach them onto my notes.

Most of the participants used various types of equipment, described by Crux (1991) as compensatory supports, such as computers, tape recorders, spelling machines such as Franklin spellers, or books on tape. Most also used various learning strategies described in the SQ3R strategy, including preview reading, structured reading (i.e., reviewing what they will focus on by using boldfaced topic headings), reading abstracts or chapter summaries that provide a "blueprint" of key information, and planning considerable amounts of time for reading. Martin, who used multiple strategies to succeed at reading, described his approach to completing his work:

For reading I need time, just give me time, and I can get it. If I read it slowly, then I can understand what is going to be discussed, whereas if you assign a book on Thursday and make it due Tuesday, I won't get much out of the book.

He also explained that he uses margin notes, as did many of the other participants:

> I check in the margin those things in the text that I think are important information. And then I go back, and I write a question out for what was discussed, and then in my own words I answer it underneath, and that way I could quiz myself.

Students also indicated they used outlining and notecards, as well as mnemonic techniques. Evan explained this way:

> If I have a list of terms or subcategories to use, I usually use mnemonics. Using the first letter of each one and make up a little saying or something like that or see if it spells half a word, I'll use that. It depends on what I'm trying to learn. I think I've found what works best for me in certain instances.

While many of the students mentioned multiple learning and compensation strategies, it is clear that each developed an individual set of strategies that enabled him or her to succeed. For some participants, this system included various study strategies, organizing their time to enable them to find the large blocks they needed to complete their reading, and analyzing their own difficulties to be able to overcome them. Arthur explained his system by elaborating on the planning that he learned to use in UPLD:

> Well, I'm better at planning. If you want to go over the major things that enabled me to improve my grades at school, there is the untimed test time for the testing accommodations.
>   There was planning and organizing. I now carry a calendar around, and I go through all my syllabi and plan out when the exams are and what reading has to be done. I don't always get it all done. Right now I'm behind in a couple classes. But, I know what I need to do and I have it in little pieces . . . chunking, the term that they use. Keeping me from getting overwhelmed, if I have a list of eight chapters that I need to do by next Saturday, that's overwhelming for me. I have to break it up; I have to start with chapter one. If the chapters are really long, I do sections of chapters, stuff like that. Self-awareness, I guess that was a big thing, knowing how long I need to do something. When I started the program, I couldn't plan out how long I needed to read a chapter. How long I needed to work on something. Now, I take note of the time it takes me, so I get a better idea of how to plan.

Most of the participants also indicated that they could not be employed during the academic year because of the amount of time necessary for them to complete their academic work. One participant, who worked at a job related to his passion and avocation, bicycling, took only two courses in several semesters when the nature of the courses was particularly demanding in light of his learning disability; most others work only in the summer.

Several of the participants also mentioned what may be labeled an "underground network," a system of checking with other students about professors from whom they should take classes. They tried to find professors who were fair, who would make the necessary accommodations for students with learning disabilities, and whose lectures were keyed to the assigned text. The option of selecting these professors was possible because participants attended a large university. At a smaller college, fewer choices exist. Joe indicated that selection of professors was a major "success" strategy for him: "I learned to cope by getting the right teachers, those who let me compensate for my learning disability."

Three themes emerged relating to compensation and learning strategies used by successful high-ability university students with learning disabilities. First, each participant developed a system that was unique to the nature of his or her disability, his or her personal styles and preferences, and the most appropriate compensation strategies. Second, they applied an extraordinary amount of time, effort, and energy to their studies. Forrest described his preparation for a chemistry exam:

> For the last chemistry exam in particular. My notes run very close to the book. I went through the book. I took notes on nearly everything in the book that wasn't considered important. All the major theories of people. On the six chapters, I took 12 pages of notes, and then I went through that, and what I did is, I studied that, and then I rewrote everything that I didn't feel like I had the first time. I would just do that until I knew everything backwards and forwards, and then I went through the notes in the book, and anything I hadn't studied already in the book and the notes. I just wrote down what to study, but I spend days of doing that amount of studying. It wasn't just taking the notes. I didn't count that as just studying. I would finish reading the chapters about a week before the exam, and spend a couple of days taking notes on the exam, for the exam from the book. I'd say I probably put in 30 hours or more studying for the exam. I mean that. . . . I'd put in the days before the exam, I'd put in three to five hours a day for at least four to five days in a row, at least four days in a row.

The third theme was the degree of comfort the participants gained using the various learned compensation strategies. A continuum existed relating to the adjustment these students experienced around the use of compensation strategies for their learning problems. Forrest and Diane believed they were "cheating" or not really working if they used reasonable accommodations, such as extended time for tests and the use of a word processor for exams. Diane was constantly told in elementary and secondary school that if she would only work and study harder, she could overcome her learning problems. Accordingly, in the university setting, she continued to believe that asking for help was analogous to admitting she hadn't worked hard enough. Forrest initially felt the same way:

> If I got an A, I wanted to get it under the same circumstances as every-body else. Because I felt like maybe I was cheating in my work if I had an advantage that they [other students] didn't. After a while, though, I realized that I am at a slight disadvantage, anyway, so it [using extra time in exams] just balances out. Now that doesn't bother me at all any-more; and, like I said, with the extra time in exams, sometimes I use it. I am always prepared to use [this accommodation], like I will get there early, or I will have the option to stay late.

Approximately half of the students used services provided in the UPLD and various learned compensation strategies easily and without guilt, while still others analyzed and reflected about why they needed help and why it may be difficult to request assistance. Peggy noted this:

> I think that the hardest thing is to . . . know when I need more help and when I can do it on my own. I am an individual, and I don't like some-one else doing things for me, or even doing things with me, and it was very hard to get to the point to say, "I need help learning to memorize things." I want to be able to do it on my own, and I was constantly being told that I was smart enough to do it on my own, and it was frustrating to realize that I have to do extra to get to [the] same point that other people can get to just by reading it.

Although many of the students mentioned multiple learning and compen-sation strategies, it is clear that each selected the particular strategies that worked best for him or her. For each participant, an individual system, defined by Denckla (1989) as executive functions, was developed, sometimes intuitively by the individual student and sometimes collaboratively by the student and a learning specialist from the UPLD, which enabled him or her to succeed using a combination of compensation and learning strategies.

Self-Perceived Strengths Including Work Habits and Flexibility

Another strategy for success, one developed by almost all of the partici-pants, was the acquisition of excellent work habits in response to difficulties. Dedication was needed to succeed in a challenging university system, and many students emphasized their strong belief in their own potential and a will-ingness to go to great lengths to realize that potential. The majority believed their capacity for hard work was their greatest asset. These students learned how to work hard because of their learning disabilities, as was clear in these representative comments:

I worked very hard. I would do hours of homework every night, but I am glad I learned how to do homework in high school, and so now I know how to do it here in college. (Peggy)

I was always. . . . I even consider myself now, and complain sometimes about it, but I was always the worker. I always did the gardening, or the landscaping, or the vacuuming, or the dishes. (Martin)

The determination and motivation of each of these students was quite clear in their interviews and in the corresponding interviews with their parents. Their commitment to hard work, to follow through on what they needed to accomplish, and their self-initiative often made them tired. Half of the participants experienced this feeling. Arthur explained,

It's just, you know, I just got through three big exams, stayed up to four in the morning, got up at six, and now I got to do more work. So, I need a break.

The work ethic described by the participants carried over into their employment; each had one or a number of summer jobs to defray college costs. The motivation that enabled them to work hard usually focused on obtaining a university degree. In fact, many of the participants reported that they became *more* committed to graduate because of their learning disability.

Several of the participants had to be flexible about choices and change their majors in order to succeed in a university setting. For those who must spend hours reading what students without learning disabilities can read in minutes, the pursuit of a liberal arts degree remains challenging, even with the use of compensation strategies. Some did major in liberal arts and used many of the compensation and learning strategies discussed in this article. However, other students learned to select majors in areas that enabled them to tap into their strengths and succeed without the hours of reading required in the liberal arts curriculum. Mathematics, engineering, sciences, physical therapy, and music are all areas selected for majors by this group. Evan's learning disability created problems for him in mathematics, so he altered his career goal by choosing a prelaw major:

I came into school as prebusiness and I found that my learning disability hindered me, especially in the math. And accounting, I mean, I dropped both of those classes . . . It was kind of hard, but I think I'm better prepared to handle something like [law] than the math aspect of business.

Counseling

Half of these students were deeply affected by what happened to them as children due to the discrepancy created by their high abilities and their learning disabilities. Complex emotions continue to affect many of them, and counseling may be a consideration for other students with similar problems relating to the intersection of giftedness and learning disabilities. Five sought counseling to reconcile some of the problems and mixed messages they encountered in their educational experiences. Kate, who had problems dealing with the interaction of her ability and her disability, was proud that she was going to graduate from college. She explained that her father, who had never really understood her learning disability, attended a special program with her during her senior year of high school and finally seemed to understand some of the problems she had been dealing with during school.

> When I graduated from high school, the look in his eyes. He said, "I am so proud of you for graduating, not just because you graduated, but because you are learning disabled and you graduated." Now, my goal is, I'll be the first. My brother got lazy, my sister just didn't go to college. It wasn't her thing. So I will be the first [in my family] probably to grad-uate. I don't want to just do it for my parents. That would be wonder-ful; but, yet, to get ahead you have to work, and I can do it. I can do it. I knew one girl who was learning disabled and she didn't go to college because she couldn't. She couldn't do it. I know that I do have a poten-tial, and I can do it, so I had to.

DISCUSSION

The data collected in this study indicate that some high-ability students with learning disabilities succeed in a rigorous university setting with the help of various compensation strategies. The ways they incorporated these strategies into a successful academic college or university experience warrant discussion.

Participants who were involved in an elementary or secondary program for students with learning disabilities believe that they learned during their college years most, if not all, of the compensation and learning strategies that made them successful. Unfortunately, the LD programs in which they participated in elementary and secondary school, according to the perceptions of the partici-pants and parents in this study, focused on remediation of content-related deficits or the opportunity to do homework or catch up on work missed in class instead of instruction in the compensation strategies they needed. Their partici-pation in a university program for students with learning disabilities provided their first organized opportunity for training in compensation and learning strategies, and they all believed that this postsecondary program was essential to their success.

Participants were able to resolve the conflict between their abilities and their disabilities. Some learned the compensation strategies needed to directly address their learning disabilities and become successful in an area that may have initially appeared difficult, if not impossible. Evan, for example, became a political science major despite a learning disability that hindered his skills in writing and reading. Some participants were careful to select an academic direction in which they had strengths *and* in which their success was not dependent upon the acquisition of compensation strategies or the mastery of academic content that was directly affected by their learning disabilities. For example, Peggy's musical talents led her to pursue a major in voice, thus enabling her to avoid the continued struggle to compensate for her numerous learning difficulties in verbally demanding academic areas. These options are not available to an elementary or secondary student who has either no choices or extremely limited academic choices in school. Third, the majority of participants in this study combined the two options mentioned above as they attempted to compensate for their learning disability and select a major area of concentration that fostered the use of their strengths to enhance their academic performance. For example, Colin, whose learning disability was particularly manifested in reading and writing, pursued a major in electrical and systems engineering, thereby enabling him to focus on his talents. He still had to learn compensation strategies in order to be successful, but he did not have to use them to the extent that would have been necessary had he majored in an area that primarily required reading and writing skills. Baum's (1984) observations about the importance of focusing on a talent while developing compensatory strategies are certainly affirmed by these successful adults with learning disabilities.

CONCLUSION

The creation of a personal plan for academic success varied among participants, but always included these elements: the use of carefully selected and individually necessary compensation strategies and the integration of certain executive functions that guided the students' decisions and the directions they took (or didn't take). Similar to the highly successful adults in Gerber and Reiff's research (1991), all of the successful participants shared the ability to focus on developing their talents instead of focusing on their deficits. Their university experiences often enabled them to select courses and later majors, in which their considerable potential for talent could develop.

The process of creating academic success was slightly different for each participant in this study. All 12 came from different types of families, although similarities existed. All were White, and many came from above-average socioeconomic backgrounds. One wonders what may happen to high-ability students with learning disabilities who come from culturally different backgrounds or economically disadvantaged environments. These participants also found a college academic environment in which they could succeed, but few found this type of environment in elementary or secondary school. We must hypothesize that many high-ability students who do not learn compensation strategies in an appropriate elementary or secondary school learning disability program and/or gifted program do not learn the skills necessary to succeed in elementary, secondary, or postsecondary education. Educators must reexamine the approaches used at the elementary and secondary levels to address the special education needs of high-ability students with learning disabilities. Pull-out programs that focus on remediation may be detrimental for this population. Instead, instruction in compensatory strategies and self-advocacy must be incorporated in an inclusive approach that fosters self-reliance, a critical factor in the arena of higher education.

REFERENCES

Adelman, P. B., & Vogel, S. A. (1993). Issues in program evaluation. In S. A. Vogel & P. B. Adelman (Eds.), *Success for college students with learning disabilities* (pp. 323–343). New York: Springer-Verlag.

Bandura, A. (1986). *Social foundations of thought and action.* Englewood Cliffs, NJ: Prentice-Hall.

Bandura, A. (1997). *Self-efficacy: The exercise of control.* New York: W. H. Freeman.

Baum, S. (1984). Meeting the needs of the learning disabled gifted student. *Roeper Review, 7*, 16–19.

Baum, S., & Owen, S. V. (1988). High ability/learning disabled students: How are they different? *Gifted Child Quarterly, 32*, 321–326.

Baum, S., Owen, S. V., & Dixon, J. (1991). *To be gifted and learning disabled: From definitions to practical intervention strategies.* Mansfield Center, CT: Creative Learning Press.

Borkowski, J. G., & Burke, J. E. (1996). Theories, models, and measurements of executive functioning: An information processing perspective. In G. R. Lyon & N. A. Karsnegor (Eds.), *Attention, memory, and executive function.* (pp. 235–261). Baltimore: Paul H. Brookes.

Bragstad, B. J., & Stumpf, S. M. (1987). *A guidebook for teaching: Study skills and motivation* (2nd ed.). Newton, MA: Allyn and Bacon.

Brinckerhoff, L. B., Shaw, S. F., & McGuire, J. M. (1993). *Promoting postsecondary education for students with learning disabilities: A handbook for practitioners.* Austin, TX: PRO-ED.

Brody, L. E., & Mills, C. J. (1997). Gifted children with learning disabilities: A review of the issues. *Journal of Learning Disabilities, 30*, 282–296.

Crux, S. C. (1991). *Learning strategies for adults: Compensation for learning disabilities.* Middletown, OH: Wall & Emerson.

Daniels, P. R. (1983). *Teaching the learning-disabled/gifted child.* Rockville, MD: Aspen.

Daniels, P. R. (1986). Educator urges schools to identify plan for gifted/learning disabled. *Hilltop Spectrum, 4*(2), 1–6.

Denckla, M. B. (1989). Executive function, the overlap zone between attention deficit hyperactivity disorder and learning disability. *International Pediatrics, 4*(2), 155–160.

Flavell, J. H., Miller, P. H., & Miller, S. A. (1993). *Cognitive development.* Englewood Cliffs, NJ: Prentice-Hall.

Fox, L. H., Brody, L., & Tobin, D. (1983). *Learning-disabled/gifted children: Identification and programming.* Baltimore: University Park Press.

Garner, R. (1988). Verbal-report data on cognitive and metacognitive strategies. In C. E. Weinstein, E. T. Goetz, & P. A. Alexander (Eds.), *Learning and study strategies: Issues in assessment, instruction, and evaluation* (pp. 63–74). New York: Academic Press.

Gerber, P. J., Ginsberg, R., & Reiff, H. B. (1992). Identifying alterable patterns in employment success for highly successful adults with learning disabilities. *Journal of Learning Disabilities, 25,* 475–87.

Gerber, P. J., & Reiff, H. B. (1991). *Speaking for themselves: Ethnographic interviews with adults with learning disabilities.* Ann Arbor, MI: University of Michigan Press.

Graham, S., & Harris, K. (1987). Improving composition skills of inefficient learners with self-instructional strategy training. *Topics in Language Disorders, 7,* 66–77.

Guba, E. G. (1978). *Toward a methodology of naturalistic inquiry in educational evaluation.* Los Angeles: University of California Press.

Henderson, C. (1995). *College freshmen with disabilities: A triennial statistical profile.* Washington, DC: American Council on Education.

Jacobson, V. (1984). *The gifted learning disabled.* Calumet, IN: Purdue University. (ERIC Document Reproduction Service No. ED 254 981)

Jick, T. D. (1983). Mixing qualitative and quantitative methods: Triangulation in action. In J. Van Maanen (Ed.), *Qualitative methodology* (pp. 135–148). Beverly Hills, CA: Sage Publications.

Maker, C. J. (1978). *The self-perceptions of successful handicapped scientists* Washington, DC: U.S. Department of Health, Education, and Welfare, Office of Education, Bureau of the Education for the Handicapped (Grant No. G00-7701[905])

Mayer, R. E. (1988). Learning strategies: An overview. In C. E. Weinstein, E. T. Goetz, & P. A. Alexander (Eds.), *Learning and study strategies: Issues in assessment, instruction, and evaluation* (pp. 11–22). New York: Academic Press.

McGuire, J. M., Hall, D., & Litt, A. V. (1991). A field-based study of the direct service needs of college students with learning disabilities. *Journal of College Student Development, 32,* 101–108.

McGuire, J. M., Shaw, S. F., & Anderson, P. (1992). *Guidelines for documentation of a specific learning disability.* Storrs, CT: University of Connecticut Program Guidelines.

Miller, R. V., Rzonca, C., & Snider, B. (1991). Variables related to the type of postsecondary education experience chosen by young adults with learning disabilities. *Journal of Learning Disabilities, 24*(3), 188–191.

Reis, S. M., Neu, T. W., & McGuire, J. M. (1995). *Talents in two places: Case studies of high ability students with learning disabilities who have achieved.* Storrs, CT: The National Research Center on the Gifted and Talented.

Schiff, M., Kaufman, A. S., & Kaufman, N. L. (1981). Scatter analysis of WISC-R profiles for learning disabled children with superior intelligence. *Journal of Learning Disabilities, 14,* 400–404.

Shaw, S. F., Brinckerhoff, L. C., Kistler, J. K., & McGuire, J. M. (1992). Preparing students with learning disabilities for postsecondary education: Issues and future needs. *Learning Disabilities, 2*(1), 21–26.

Shore, B. M., & Dover, A. C. (1987). Metacognition, intelligence and giftedness. *Gifted Child Quarterly, 31,* 37–39.

Spradley, J. P. (1979). *The ethnographic interview.* New York: Holt, Rinehart, and Winston.

Sternberg, R. J. (1981). A componential theory of intellectual giftedness. *Gifted Child Quarterly, 25,* 86–93.

Sternberg, R. J., & Davidson, J. E. (Eds.). (1986). *Conceptions of giftedness.* New York: Cambridge University Press.

Strauss, A. L. (1987). *Qualitative analysis for social scientists.* New York: Cambridge University Press.

Strauss, A. L., & Corbin, J. (1990). *Basics of qualitative research.* Newbury Park, CA: Sage.

Stuss, D. T., & Benson, D. F. (1986). *The frontal lobes.* New York: Raven Press.

Vail, P. (1987). *Smart kids with school problems.* New York: E. P. Dutton.

Vail, P. L. (1989). The gifted learning disabled student. In L. B. Silver (Ed.), *The assessment of learning disabilities: Preschool through adulthood* (pp. 135–160). Austin, TX: PRO-ED.

Van Maanen, J. (1983). Reclaiming qualitative research methods for organizational research. In J. Van Maanen (Ed.), *Qualitative methodology* (pp. 9–18). Beverly Hills, CA: Sage.

Whitmore, J. (1980). *Giftedness, conflict, and underachievement.* Boston: Allyn and Bacon.

Whitmore, J. R., & Maker, J. (1985). *Intellectual giftedness in disabled persons.* Rockville, MD: Aspen.

Wong, B. Y. L. (1987). How do the results of metacognitive research impact on the learning disabled student? *Learning Disability Quarterly, 10,* 189–195.

3

Gifted Students With Attention Deficits: Fact and/or Fiction?

Or, Can We See the Forest for the Trees?

Susan Baum

College of New Rochelle

F. Richard Olenchak

University of Alabama

Steven V. Owen

University of Connecticut

According to Gordon (1990), far too many high ability students are referred for problems with impulsivity, hyperactivity, and sustaining attention. Several important issues, rarely discussed in the literature on attention deficits, offer alternative hypotheses for the increasing incidence of hyperactivity and attention problems of gifted youngsters. These

Editor's Note: From Baum, S., Olenchak, F. R., & Owen, S. V. (1998). Gifted students with attention deficits: Fact and/or Fiction? Or, can we see the forest for the trees? *Gifted Child Quarterly*, 42(2), 96-104. © 1998 National Association for Gifted Children. Reprinted with permission.

include theories on emotional development and excitability of gifted students (Dabrowski, 1938; Piechowski & Colangelo, 1984), evidence of unchallenging curricula for high ability students (Reiff, 1993), implications of the multiple intelligences paradigm (Gardner, 1983), and adult reaction to students' extreme precocity (Rimm, 1994). These issues are examined in light of Barkley's theory of inhibition as it relates to the manifestation of ADHD. The issues represent environmental conditions that may cause or influence ADHD-like behaviors in high ability students. Diagnostic and intervention strategies are suggested to counteract environmental contributors to the problem.

A master of Lego™ bricks, verbally precocious Chris is failing miserably at school. Despite an estimated IQ of 172, he was retained in first grade because of failure to complete work and poor motor and social skills for his age. In second grade, his teacher referred him for special education screening because of his impulsive and disorganized behavior. Chris was diagnosed with Attention Deficit Hyperactivity Disorder (ADHD).

Referrals for attention disorders among gifted children have been growing at an unexpected rate (Webb & Latimer, 1993). Although the increases alone are troublesome, there is additional concern because of professionals' lack of clear definitions for ADHD, giftedness, creativity, and a variety of other behavioral characteristics (Cramond, 1994: Jordan, 1992; Piechowski, 1991). Diagnosis of ADHD sweeps across a number of problematic behaviors such as impulsivity and hyperactivity, in addition to a collection of deficits in concentration, persistence for tasks, organization of thinking, and focusing attention. Such varied aspects of ADHD have prompted some researchers to claim that most gifted students with learning disabilities also demonstrate behaviors associated with ADHD (M. Cherkes-Julkowski, personal communication, March 9, 1993).

Putting the Research to Use

Why is there concern about the apparent over-identification of bright, creative students with Attention Deficit Hyperactivity Disorder (ADHD)? The coincidence of ADHD and giftedness has received little exploration, particularly in light of the delicate interaction between characteristics of students and requirements of learning environments. Characteristics and behaviors can be misleading when they form the primary foundation for diagnosis of any exceptionality. Moreover, much of the information regarding ADHD has emerged from the medical and special education fields, neither of which has considerable knowledge of or expertise in giftedness.

In this article, we outline a variety of perspectives from which to consider and interpret the behaviors of gifted students who are suspected of having attention difficulties and suggest care be taken to consider a course of action based on the broadest array of options that allow for multiple hypotheses.

In addition, we offer diverse explanations for behaviors observed to foster a more holistic understanding of the students' needs and thereby increase the school's capacity to meet these needs. Rather than jumping to conclusions, educators and parents are encouraged to follow a step-by-step course of action that serves to rule out alternate hypotheses prior to referral for ADHD behaviors. Environmental modalities and strategies must be considered and assessed for behavioral effects by conducting comprehensive observations of classroom activities, curricular and pacing adaptations, and school efforts to reinforce creativity as well as to develop individual talent.

The most frequently prescribed intervention for ADHD is medication in the methylphenidate family, usually Ritalin-AE. Medications are usually successful in controlling behavior, but they are also suspected to inhibit creativity and intellectual curiosity in bright children. Anecdotal reports tell of gifted youngsters being "cured of their giftedness" in an effort to help them attend to schoolwork. As Cramond (1994) put it, "perhaps we are lucky that medication was not available to stop the daydreams of Robert Frost and Frank Lloyd Wright" (p. 205). No conclusive research exists to explain the impact of such medication on various thought processes, including those related to potentially creative, productive thinking. Perhaps even more worrisome is that the behaviors thought to signal a disorder might sometimes be the result of an environment where bright but reluctant youngsters are expected to conform to a sluggish and boring curriculum.

The predicament of inattentive gifted youth has several important implications. First, the loss of valuable human resources comes at a time when the world depends increasingly on its brightest and most creative youth to assist in resolving the problems of tomorrow. If we cannot design appropriate interventions that will nurture human potential, much of the world's best human capital will never reach its potential. A second concern is for lost achievement. Unfortunately, even when medication is appropriate to assist in behavior management, underachievement often continues (Lind & Olenchak, 1995). School administrators occasionally exacerbate the situation by viewing ADHD purely as a medical problem, thereby absolving themselves, teachers, and school curricula from responsibility. Parents, too, can excuse their child's inappropriate behaviors rather than providing the support and structure some of these students need to practice academic and behavioral self-regulation (Zimmerman, Bonner, & Kovach, 1996). Medical professionals admit that if schools were more receptive to individual learning needs of students and were more cognizant of ADHD and its various treatment options, a number of children would not need medication (Barkley, 1990). Educators who are successful with bright but active youngsters argue that schools should be held accountable for providing appropriate educational options for these students (Reiff, 1993). Whether medical or educational, the dilemmas are enormous for families confronted with rearing bright children who have ADHD. A spokesperson from the Association for the Education of Gifted Underachieving Students reported that the majority of inquiries received are from frustrated parents of gifted/ADHD students seeking information and strategies to help their youngsters (L. Baldwin, personal communication, November 12, 1996). The two excerpts that follow illustrate the frustration and pain faced by the parents of bright students whose school experiences have been dismal:

1. My son is 15 and has just been diagnosed with attention deficit disorder without hyperactivity. He has been steadily failing subjects since seventh grade even though his IQ is 130. We need help to restore his self-esteem and confidence. He has shown moments of brilliance since he was little, especially in any art or spatial design activity such as building with Legos™ and other structures. But any real blossoming has been shut down by his feelings of failure and years of people—teachers, counselors, and yes, his parents—telling him he is being lazy. We need help in learning how to parent so we are helpful and not harmful to our son.

2. I am a parent of two children, a girl of 15 and a boy of 12, both of whom have tested in the gifted range of intelligence and both of whom have some learning disabilities. Both have been diagnosed as having an attention deficit disorder. My daughter has poor organizational skills as well as a memory weakness and weak fine-motor integration skills. My son also has difficulty in reading with weaknesses in decoding. I am looking for ways in which I can circumvent their disabilities and stimulate them intellectually. . . . It has been difficult getting the schools to recognize their difficulties. Some teachers have been cooperative and others have not. The school system doesn't recognize their attention deficit disorder as a disability. So much time is being wasted trying to find the right people to help. The process has been trial and error without success (L. Emerick, personal communication, April 17, 1994).

Contemporary educators do not seem to have appropriate strategies, knowledge, or confidence in providing an appropriate education for gifted students with learning and attention difficulties. As mentioned by one parent, some districts dodge their legal responsibility for providing an appropriate education for such students. Although the medical profession has long recommended medication as a primary approach to the problem, educators are provided little direction about the nature and types of educational solutions that are also required.

The most serious concern is that gifted behavior is sacrificed for more manageable behavior in some creative, bright students who are medicated for ADHD. Highly able students with problems in attention, hyperactivity, and self-regulation remain at risk for developing their potential. However, it remains unclear whether these attention deficit behaviors are due to a neurological problem affecting learning, are the result of a learning environment inappropriate for such exceptional learners, or are a combination of both. The complexity of the problem motivates the development of a bio-psycho-social systems model to improve the theory, research, and educational response. Such a model should help to keep many gifted learners from falling through the cracks of the floorboards scaffolding the educational bureaucracy.

In this article, we explore unique issues of attention deficit disorders among gifted students and offer alternate explanations for the occurrence of those behaviors among some students. We first distinguish among three groups of students who demonstrate behaviors associated with ADHD: (a) students whose learning and attention problems stem, for the most part, from a neurochemical disorder; (b) those whose behaviors are mostly brought about, and perhaps intensified, by the learning environment; and (c) those who fall into both of the preceding categories.

In addition, suggestions are offered for determining whether the behaviors are primarily environmental, essentially neurological, or both. Finally, we share an approach our research has found to be particularly helpful for combating ADHD-like behaviors that are precipitated by the environment.

WHAT IS AN ATTENTION DEFICIT DISORDER?

Children with Attention Deficit Hyperactivity Disorder (ADHD), according to the fourth edition of the *Diagnostic and Statistical Manual of Mental Disorders* (*DSM-IV*; American Psychiatric Association, 1994), have problems sustaining situation-appropriate attention. These problems can include hyperactivity, alertness, arousal, and distractibility. Some researchers claim that the attention problems are exacerbated by tasks that are dull, repetitive, and boring (Barkley, 1990; Luk, 1985). Impulsivity, academic difficulties, and poor motor skills are other behaviors characterizing children with ADHD. Children with ADHD frequently fail to complete assignments in school or at home, exhibit disruptive behavior in the classroom, and have difficulty relating to their classmates. A majority of these students have learning deficits in spelling, math, reading, and handwriting (Barkley, 1990).

Despite current media fascination, this syndrome is not a recent invention. It had been noted in psychiatric literature as early as the mid-1800s. Its emergence in this century began with the appearance of Strauss and Lehtinen's (1947) book, *Psychopathology and Education of the Brain-Injured Child*. In the 1950s and 1960s, children who were of at least average ability and who exhibited certain symptoms were identified as having Strauss' Syndrome, or minimal brain damage, because theorists and researchers of that era believed the behaviors represented some injury to the brain. Characteristics associated with Strauss' Syndrome included the following behaviors:

1. Erratic and inappropriate behavior on mild provocation;

2. Increased motor activity;

3. Poor organization of behavior;

4. Distractibility of more than ordinary degree under ordinary conditions;

5. Persistent faulty perceptions;

6. Persistent hyperactivity; and

7. Awkwardness and consistently poor motor performance (Stevens & Birch, 1957).

In the 1970s, professionals dropped the brain injury-behavior link because these connections were virtually impossible to verify, and they focused instead on labeling the set of behaviors as the Hyperactive Child Syndrome. In the early 1980s, psychologists redefined the disorder by de-emphasizing the role of hyperactivity as the primary symptom of the disorder and elevating the importance of one's ability to sustain attention and to control impulses. Some students, it was noted, were not particularly hyperactive but rather seemed to "drift off" during lectures, reading assignments, and written tasks. This led to the emergence of two terms to describe these children as those who had either Attention Deficit Disorder (ADD) with Hyperactivity or ADD without Hyperactivity (American Psychiatric Association, 1980).

Today, researchers have returned to an earlier focus by re-labeling the syndrome as Attention Deficit Hyperactivity Disorder (ADHD). This label reflects the position that hyperactivity along with problems sustaining attention and controlling impulses are the primary symptoms of the disorder. Theorists do not deny that some children experience attention deficits without hyperactivity, but they argue it may be an altogether different syndrome (Carlson, 1986).

Many theories about the causes of the problem are currently being investigated. There is consensus about a genetic and physiological predisposition to the disorder (Barkley, 1995; M. Cherkes-Julkowski, personal communication, February 3, 1995). However, researchers currently are exploring a variety of hypotheses in an attempt to explain how the environment interacts with the individual to bring about manifestations of the disorder. Some theories focus on the notion that individuals with ADHD have an extraordinary need for stimulation (Zental, 1985) or are easily confused with energetic, highly creative people (Cramond, 1994). These hypotheses focus on the behavior-environment relationship: when environmental stimuli decrease, hyperactivity and inattention increase as a means of self-stimulation to compensate for the "boring environment." Others cite motivational causes for the behaviors (Haenlein & Caul, 1987). These researchers claim the lack of sustained attention owes to the individual's need for excessive reinforcement both in kind and frequency. They claim that when a task does not have strong intrinsic appeal, it cannot hold the ADHD learner's attention. Some argue that children with ADHD show poor self-regulation of behavior, thus failing to meet the demands expected in certain situations (Routh, 1978). Usually these situations are highly structured and require adherence to a specific set of social rules (Barkley, 1990).

The important issue is that, although each of these hypotheses has implications for intervention, they cannot be considered in the absence of theories explaining the unique qualities of gifted students and how those characteristics modify conceptions of ADHD in the gifted population. Unfortunately, the majority of researchers and professionals involved in the area of ADHD has little contact with experts in the social and emotional development of the gifted child. Likewise, few theorists or practitioners in gifted education are familiar with the literature of medicine, psychiatry, or special education. This lack of paradigm sharing limits the ability of concerned professionals to offer complete and appropriate diagnoses or effective strategies for addressing the problems of gifted youngsters with ADHD.

ALTERNATIVE PERSPECTIVES

According to Gordon (1990), far too many gifted students are referred for problems with hyperactivity and attention. There are several important perspectives rarely discussed in the ADHD literature that may help to explain why some gifted youngsters have difficulty in adapting to traditional schooling and may, therefore, be especially susceptible to attention problems. A variety of new research findings, research-based theories, or applications of old theories to the gifted population present opportunities for better understanding ADHD and its relationship to gifted youngsters. These include the emotional development of gifted students, curricular and pacing issues, the nature of intelligence, and adult response to child precocity. We turn now to these alternative perspectives.

Emotional Development of Gifted Students

The evolving theory of emotional development and developmental potential of gifted individuals (e.g., Dabrowski & Piechowski, 1977; Piechowski & Colangelo, 1984; Olenchak, 1994; Piechowski, 1991; Silverman, 1993) offers a different lens for examining the growing occurrence of hyperactivity and attention problems in gifted youngsters. Dabrowski's theory of positive disintegration aims to explain qualitative differences of human development. He proposed that gifted individuals had "increased psychic excitabilities" that predicted extraordinary achievement (Nelson, 1989). The concept of overexcitabilities has been described as:

> an expanded and intensified manner of experiencing in the psychomotor, sensual, intellectual, imaginational, and emotional areas . . . As personal traits, overexcitabilities are often not valued socially. Being viewed instead as nervousness, hyperactivity, neurotic temperament, excessive emotionality and emotional intensity that most people find uncomfortable at close range. (Piechowski & Colangelo, 1984, p. 81)

Relevant to this discussion is Piechowski and Colangelo's (1984) description of psychomotor overexcitability. They defined the trait as "an organic excess of energy or excitability of the neuromuscular system. It may manifest itself as a love of movement for its own sake, rapid speech, pursuit of intense physical activities, impulsiveness, restlessness, pressure for action, drivedness, the capacity for being active and energetic" (p. 81).

Piechowski and Colangelo (1984, p. 83) gave examples from gifted adolescents describing their psychomotoric overexcitability needs. One young man explained, "When I'm around my friends, I usually come up with so much energy I don't know where it came from. Also when I am bored, I get sudden urges and lots of energy . . . [in school] I use this energy to goof off." Another student reported, "Like when I've been doing a long homework assignment. . . . I suddenly get the urge to shoot baskets or ride my bike."

This energy seems to come as much from boredom as from excitement of new ideas. Some students report the need to dance to some music before sitting down to write about some new idea or before finally mastering a complex piece in music. Cruickshank (1963, 1967, 1977), whose seminal work with hyperactive students is well known, came to assess hyperactivity and extreme sensitivity to the environment as positive characteristics in bright children rather than as problematic behavior. When such gifted children appear impulsive, it simply may be their extra urge to explore their world (Piechowski, 1991). Their curiosity and desire for knowledge can take precedence over the school's need for a prescribed curriculum locked in time, sequence, and space. In this sense, the regular classroom can be too restrictive for students predisposed to "overexcitabilities."

Inappropriate Curriculum and Pacing

Another set of factors that may contribute to school-related problems among gifted students involves issues of curricula and instruction. As has been shown, problems with hyperactivity, attention, and impulsivity increase when the curriculum is perceived as routine and dull; consequently, certain gifted children are placed at risk for failure. Research has shown that many bright students are not being taught at their instructional level and, by definition, do not require the usual amount of repetition to master many skills (Gallagher, 1990; Reis et al., 1993; Stanley, 1978).

The results of a major national study revealed that much of the regular curriculum is redundant for gifted students (Reis et al., 1993). When as much as 60% of the curriculum was eliminated, gifted students exceeded or equaled achievement levels of matched students who were required to complete the regular curriculum. Although these findings bode ill for bright students in general, consider the plight of those who tend to be predisposed to seeking greater levels of stimulation from the environment. They are automatically at odds with the expectations schools have for students to be neat, docile, quiet for extended periods, and interested in what the teacher is teaching.

Chris, the child mentioned at the beginning of this article, is a case in point, He was often punished for blurting out answers during whole class lessons. For example, when the teacher asked the class to figure out the answer to a problem on the chalkboard, Chris jumped out of his seat, ran to the board, and solved the problem before anyone else had a chance to respond. His teacher cited this instance as extreme impulsivity; her lack of understanding of Chris' needs produced a misinterpretation of his behavior. In short, gifted children who are active are placed in double jeopardy. On one hand, these children have an intrinsic need to discover, understand, and master the curriculum; they need to be actively engaged in learning. However, when school tasks are mysteriously frustrating or not meaningful and the environment is unfriendly, the student may avoid the aversion by searching for solace through optimal arousal elsewhere. This "elsewhere" is often in their mind's eye where daydreams are far more arousing than the school curriculum (Baum, Owen, & Dixon, 1991). For some students, it is inventing a need to visit the school nurse who may have developed a positive and stimulating relationship with these articulate, intellectually fascinating youngsters. For still others, disrupting the class routine in any way possible remains a good primary means of attention and arousal (Baum, 1985; Lind & Olenchak, 1995).

Application of Multiple Intelligence Theory

Gardner's Theory of Multiple Intelligences (1983, 1993) offers yet another hypothesis for understanding the complexity of attention disorders. Denying a unitary conception of intelligence, Gardner has claimed that students' potential strengths may be in one or more of eight intellectual domains: verbal, logical-mathematical, spatial, kinesthetic, musical, naturalistic, interpersonal, and intrapersonal. Because school is mostly about verbal and logical-mathematical abilities, other ways of knowing and communicating are not only restricted but often devalued. Many gifted youngsters who are not achieving in school have exceptional spatial abilities (Baum et al., 1991; Dixon, 1983; Olenchak, 1995; Silverman, 1989). Often these students are described by their teachers as disruptive, off-task and deviously adept at avoiding unpleasant tasks. However, when creating with Lego™ bricks, repairing a motor, or drawing cartoon characteristics, these same students can be remarkably calm, focused, and persistent (Baum et al., 1991).

It appears that when some hyperactive students are encouraged to learn and communicate in an area of strength (usually a non-verbal intelligence), even boring tasks are accomplished without accompanying behavioral problems. For example, some upper elementary students with severe attention disorders who were found to have potential talent in dance or music were selected to participate in a federally funded program designed to recognize and nurture those talents (Baum, Owen, & Oreck, 1996). Their classroom or special education teachers were amazed at the ability of students to attend to tasks during the dance or music classes. Ray, a fourth grader whose teachers described as "needing excessive attention, being all over the place, and lacking ability to concentrate," was a different child in dance class. "I could not believe the way he stays on tasks, focuses his attention on the dance teacher, and is willing to do a particular movement again and again until he does it correctly," exclaimed this same teacher. Could it be that students with attention-related disorders are best served in an environment that incorporates and values alternate modes of thinking and communicating? Perhaps attention deficits are connected to specific intelligences, an idea that has not yet been investigated.

Adults' Response to Child Precocity

There is evidence that some adults (e.g., teachers and parents) may be intimidated or overwhelmed by the precocity of gifted youngsters and, as a result, may fail to exercise control over the child's behavior (Rimm, 1994). Such adults may underestimate the ability of these students to regulate their own behavior. In these cases, not only is the child excused for misbehavior, but their misbehavior is reinforced by adult assertions that the child cannot control it.

TESTING THE HYPOTHESES: UNDERSTANDING THE ISSUES

In truth, there are probably multiple factors and combinations of factors contributing to the difficulties that some gifted students experience while attending to and controlling their behavior. Barkley (1995) has suggested a theory that hints at the delicate interaction between the characteristics of the students and the requirements of the environment. He argues that ADHD is best understood in terms of inhibition, which he views as a trait. Everyone thus falls somewhere along a continuum of extreme inhibition to no inhibition (see Figure 1). Excessive inhibition can effectively paralyze one from engaging in life activities; at the other end, the absence of inhibition can result in reckless behavior, a lack of impulse control, and inability to delay gratification. Barkley defines deficits of attention as a special case of the latter extreme. For Barkley, ADHD is, consequently, a portion of the inhibition trait. We will argue that, although such traits are viewed as enduring dispositions, there are dependable conditions that will cause the trait to appear or disappear in human behavior.

Figure 1   Interpretation of Barkley's Trait Theory of ADHD as It Applies to Giftedness

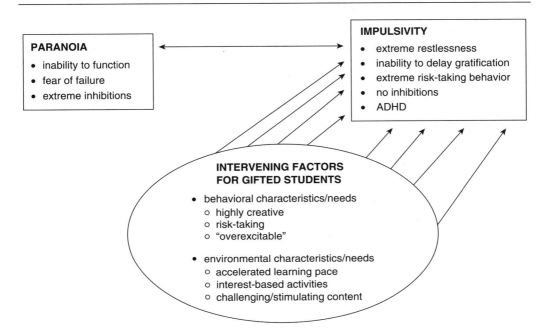

In short, the trait lies beneath the surface, but the behaviors it manifests depend, in part, on the environment. For example, a usually self-regulated student under pressure of an important exam can become more inhibited and fearful than usual or even lose concentration altogether.

Creative people with high energy and ability are less inhibited and more likely to take risks. Because they are highly motivated to accomplish their own goals, they may create their own rules and be unwilling to postpone their agenda. Curiosity and urge for stimulation drives highly creative persons to take even more risks than customary and to forge ahead with little consideration of consequences. Likewise, students with high abilities are driven to engage in new learning and challenges. These qualities place gifted and creative people on the low inhibition side of the continuum (see Figure 1). When the environment is too restrictive and inhibits the natural energy of such students, they find themselves being pushed toward a more extreme end of the continuum. At that point, the behavior of these students may resemble that of a smaller number of people who truly suffer from ADHD due to neurological or chemical imbalances. Once individuals' behavior dictates placement at this end of the continuum, regardless of the cause (environmental or neurological), they have minimal skills or capacities to regulate their own behavior without medical, cognitive, or psychological intervention.

Thus, to make an appropriate referral for ADHD behaviors, it is important to consider the effects of the environment on the student's behavior. In other words, we must estimate to what extent traditional school environments and curricula serve as gateways for the emergence of attention deficit-like behaviors. Only then can we be confident that the ADHD behaviors are primarily the result of a neurological or chemical imbalance.

To rule out alternate hypotheses, we need to analyze and modify the environment that may be responsible for prompting the behavior. If changes in the classroom—including curricula and instruction—result in improved student attention and behavior, more intrusive and ineffectual interventions can be avoided. We suggest the following strategies to assist in this evaluation:

1. Observe and document under which circumstances the child has difficulty in attending to tasks and otherwise performing acceptably.

2. Consider Gardner's notion of multiple intelligences; are there adaptations of curricular presentations (e.g., visual or kinesthetic instead of verbal) that might capture the student's attention?

3. Observe the student's behavior in different learning environments to estimate the optimal conditions for learning.

4. Observe parent-child and teacher-child interactions to ascertain whether limits are set, if strategies for self-regulation are provided, and whether the student actually is able to self-regulate.

5. Observe the child at different times of the day to decide to what degree the student's creativity is appreciated, reinforced, or allowed expression.

6. Investigate whether there is any effort to develop the student's gifts or talents; if so, how does the student behave during appropriate talent development activities?

7. Pretest the student to assess instructional levels and evaluate appropriate curricular pacing.

The results of these observations can suggest specific strategies that can minimize learning obstacles facing the student. These observations should provide information that will help to discern:

1. which students will profit solely from environmental intervention like Chris, described earlier, who, when the curriculum was differentiated and his gift was accommodated, made his disruptive, inattentive behavior disappear.

2. which students will require chemical intervention like Brad, whose impulsivity in social interactions caused great difficulty for him. However, once on medication his behavior greatly improved, and he was able to develop social relationships.

3. which students will need both types of interventions like Adam, whose extreme giftedness and hyperactivity combined to make school an

abysmal experience. In this case, both medication and acceleration were needed to address his problems.

Unfortunately, current remedies for the vast majority of bright students with ADHD-like behaviors typically encompass plans for medication and behavior modification, with little attention extended to curricula and instruction. In fact, many strategies used in gifted education have been found to accommodate the needs of such children in a more positive, less invasive, and more appropriate manner. For example, several research projects have successfully used talent development or attention to students' gifts, abilities, or intelligences as an intervention for promoting academic success for gifted students at-risk, including high ability students with attention and learning problems (Baum et al., 1996; Baum, Renzulli, & Hébert, 1994; Neu & Baum, 1995; Olenchak, 1994, 1995). These studies showed that modifications in curriculum, pacing, and instructional strategies had positive effects on increasing student attention and in improving self-regulatory behavior and achievement. Offering high levels of challenge and problem solving opportunities, especially in areas of the students' talents and interests, resulted in student's willful engagement and sustained interest in learning activities. Often when teacher talk was minimized so that students were allowed to explore their environments and to engage actively in learning and inquiry, no symptoms of ADHD surfaced.

Consider Bryan, an eighth grader, described by his teachers as a "serious behavior problem, socially inept, impulsive, and never completing assignments." In contrast, Bryan himself reported frequently cooking up creative ideas but then usually losing interest in them. He became interested in rewriting a court simulation used in the eighth grade civics course because he thought the original simulation was "stupid." Bryan was able to test out of civics because he already knew most of the content for the year and, thus, was able to use that time to work with the enrichment teacher on his project. Armed with a management plan that reduced the overall project into smaller, sequenced steps, a computer, and information from interviews and observations he had conducted about trials, Bryan began his writing. As he pursued this project, he thought of ideas for two novels, both of which he began to write along with the simulation. Working on three projects at once provided Bryan with an outlet for his "overexcitabilities," as his mind was often bombarded with exciting new ideas for new schemes as he worked on the law simulation. During the course of working on these projects, Bryan realized he was better able to concentrate on his writing while "plugged into his music," which is often the case for students strong in kinesthetic intelligence (M. Cherkes-Julkowski, personal communication, May 21, 1995). He spent marathon sessions on his computer while wearing his Sony Walkman, and he negotiated with his English teacher to allow him to complete classroom writing assignments in the computer lab. His teacher noticed that Bryan not only completed all assignments but improved his writing substantially. By the end of the school year, the three projects were completed, his grades and behavior improved, and he began to set higher goals for achievement for the following year.

Should Bryan have been "cured" from working on multiple projects? Should he have been required to sit in a civics class when he already knew much of the material? Should students be asked to consume knowledge only for the sake of knowledge, or can they also be provided with opportunities to solve problems and learn skills within a meaningful context?

Again the questions must be posed: Are observed ADHD behaviors primarily the result of a neurological difficulty or a neurochemical imbalance that must be treated with medication and therapy? Do ADHD behaviors dissipate when educational programs are carefully designed to meet the needs of individual students? Or, finally, does effective intervention require both chemical and environmental change?

TOWARD ANSWERS

As the frequency of school disabilities attributed to attention deficits continues to soar, there are increasing reasons to believe that many bright youngsters claimed to suffer from ADHD and other problems of concentration may be misdiagnosed. The result of treating one circumstance (giftedness) as if it were another (attention problems), or of failing to serve the gift in lieu of remedying the weakness, may produce far greater academic, social, and emotional problems than those related to ADHD. It is essential for educational practitioners and diagnosticians to consider the array of alternate hypotheses under-girding student behaviors before developing treatment plans. Diagnoses—whether educational, psychological, or medical—are sometimes unequivocal, sometimes unreliable, and sometimes hardly more than guesses. If a child's actual needs serve as the primary rudder for steering the intervention, then all reasonable options should be entertained before formulating solutions. Caution must be taken to consider aspects of each student's case individually and to formulate a course of action based on the broadest array of options that allow for multiple hypotheses. Otherwise, educators and parents take the risk of discouraging that which should be nurtured and of de-emphasizing that which deserves accentuation. To conclude that all students who satisfy certain diagnostic criteria alone ipso facto suffer from attention disabilities is tantamount to ignoring individuality.

REFERENCES

American Psychological Association. (1980). *Diagnostic and statistical manual of mental disorders* (3rd ed.). Washington, DC: Author.

American Psychological Association. (1994). *Diagnostic and statistical manual of mental disorders* (4th ed.), Washington, DC: Author.

Barkley, R. A. (1989). Attention deficit hyperactivity disorder. In E. Mash & R. A. Barkley (Eds.), *Treatment of childhood disorders*. New York: The Guilford Press.

Barkley, R. A. (1990). *Attention deficit hyperactivity disorder: A handbook to diagnosing and treatment*. New York: Guilford Press.

Barkley, R. A. (1995, May). *A new theory of ADHD*. Paper presented at the International Conference on Research and Practice in Attention Deficit Disorder, Jerusalem, Israel.

Baum, S. (1985). *Learning disabled students with superior cognitive abilities: A validation study of descriptive behaviors*. Unpublished doctoral dissertation, University of Connecticut, Storrs, CT.

Baum, S. M., Owen, S. V., & Dixon, J. (1991). *To be gifted and learning disabled: From identification to practical intervention strategies*. Mansfield Center, CT: Creative Learning Press.

Baum, S. M., Owen, S. V., & Oreck, B. (1996). Talent beyond words: Identification of potential talent in dance and music in elementary students. *Gifted Child Quarterly, 40*, 93–102.

Baum, S. M., Renzulli, J. S., & Hébert, T. P. (1994). Reversing underachievement: Stories of success. *Educational Leadership, 52*, 48–53.

Carlson, C. (1986). Attention deficit disorder without hyperactivity: A review of preliminary experimental evidence. In B. Lahey & A. Kazdin (Eds.), *Advances in clinical child psychology* (pp. 3–48). New York: Plenum Press.

Cramond, B. (1994). Attention-deficit hyperactivity disorder and creativity: What is the connection? *Journal of Creative Behavior, 28*, 193–209.

Cruickshank, W. (1963). *Psychology of exceptional children and youth* (2nd ed.). Englewood Cliffs, NJ: Prentice Hall.

Cruickshank, W. (1967). *The brain-injured child in home, school, and community*. Syracuse, NY: Syracuse University Press.

Cruickshank, W. (1977). Myths and realities in learning disabilities. *Journal of Learning Disabilities, 10*, 51–58.

Dabrowski, K. (1938). Typy wzmozonej pobudliwosci: psychicnej (Types of increased psychic excitability). *Biul. Inst. Hig. Psychicznej, 1*(3–4), 3–26.

Dabrowski, K., & Piechowski, M. M. (1977). *Theory of levels of emotional development* (Vols. 1 & 2). Oceanside, NY: Dabor Science.

Dixon, J. (1983). *The spatial child*. Springfield, IL: Charles C. Thomas.

Gallagher, J. (1990). *Teaching the gifted child* (3rd ed.). Boston: Allyn & Bacon.

Gardner, H. (1983). *Frames of mind: The theory of multiple intelligences*. New York: Basic Books.

Gardner, H. (1993). *Multiple intelligences: The theory in practice*. New York: Basic Books.

Gordon, M. (1990, May). *The assessment and treatment of ADHD/Hyperactivity*. Keynote Address, annual meeting of New York Association for Children with Learning Disabilities, Syracuse, New York.

Haenlein, M., & Caul, W. F. (1987). Attention deficit disorder with hyperactivity: A specific hypothesis of reward dysfunction. *Journal of the American Academy of Child and Adolescent Psychiatry, 26*, 356–362.

Jordan, D. R. (1992). *Attention deficit disorder* (2nd ed.). Austin, TX: Pro-Ed.

Lind, S., & Olenchak, F. R. (1995, March). *ADD/ADHD and giftedness: What should educators do?* Paper presented at the eighth annual conference of the Association for the Education of Gifted Underachieving Students, Birmingham, AL.

Luk, S. (1985). Direct observation studies of hyperactive behaviors. *Journal of the American Academy of Child Psychiatry, 24*, 338–344.

Nelson, K. C. (1989). Dabrowski's theory of positive disintegration. *Advanced Development, 1*, 1–14.

Neu, T., & Baum, S. (1995, April). *Project High Hopes: Developing talent in gifted students with special needs*. Paper presented at the annual conference of the Council for Exceptional Children, Indianapolis, IN.

Olenchak, F. R. (1994). Talent development: Accommodating the social and emotional needs of secondary gifted/learning disabled students. *Journal of Secondary Gifted Education, 5*(3), 40–52.

Olenchak, F. R. (1995). Effects of enrichment on gifted/learning disabled students. *Journal for the Education of the Gifted, 18*, 385–399.

Piechowski, M. M. (1991). Emotional development and emotional giftedness. In N. Colangelo & G. Davis (Eds.), *Handbook of gifted education*. Needham Heights, MA: Allyn & Bacon.

Piechowski, M. M., & Colangelo, N. (1984). Developmental potential of the gifted. *Gifted Child Quarterly, 28*, 80–88.

Reiff, S. F. (1993). *How to reach and teach ADD/ADHD children*. West Nyack, NY: Center for Applied Research in Education.

Reis, S. M., Westberg, K. L., Kulikowich, J., Caillard, F., Hébert, T., Plucker, J., Purcell, J. H., Rogers, J. B., & Smist, J. M. (1993). *Why not let high ability students start school in January? The curriculum compacting study.* (Research Monograph No. 93106). Storrs, CT: The National Research Center on the Gifted and Talented.

Rimm, S. B. (1994). *Keys to parenting the gifted child*. Hauppauge, NY: Barron's.

Routh, D. K. (1978). Hyperactivity. In P. Magrab (Ed.), *Psychological management of pediatric problems* (pp. 3–48). Baltimore: University Press.

Silverman, L. K. (1989). Invisible gifts, invisible handicaps. *Roeper Review, 22*, 34–42.

Silverman, L. K. (1993). The gifted individual. In L.K. Silverman (Ed.), *Counseling the gifted and talented*. Denver, CO: Love Publishing.

Stanley, J. (1978). Identifying and nurturing the intellectually gifted. In R. E. Clasen & B. Robinson (Eds.), *Simple gifts*. Madison, WI: University of Wisconsin.

Stevens, G., & Birch, J. (1957). A proposal for clarification of the terminology used to describe brain-injured children. *Exceptional Children, 23*, 346–349.

Strauss, A. E., & Lehtinen, L. (1947). *Psychopathology and education of the brain-injured child*. New York: Grune & Stratton.

Webb, J. T., & Latimer, D. (1993, July). *ADHD and children who are gifted* (ERIC Document No. EDO-EC-93-5). Reston, VA: Council for Exceptional Children.

Zental, S. (1985). A context for hyperactivity. In K. Gadow (Ed.), *Advances in learning and behavioral disabilities* (pp. 278–343). Greenwich, CT: JAI Press.

Zimmerman, B., Bonner, S., & Kovach, R. (1996). *Developing self-regulated learners: Beyond achievement to self-efficacy*. Washington, DC: American Psychological Association.

4

Gifted Children With Asperger's Syndrome

Maureen Neihart

Billings, Montana

Asperger's Syndrome is a pervasive developmental disorder characterized by deficits in social communication and by repetitive patterns of behaviors or interests. It is observed in some gifted children. The author proposes that gifted children with Asperger's Syndrome may not be identified because their unusual behaviors may be wrongly attributed to either their giftedness or to a learning disability. The article discusses ways in which Asperger's Syndrome might be missed in gifted children and proposes guidelines for differentiating characteristics of giftedness from characteristics of Asperger's Syndrome.

Asperger's Syndrome is a pervasive developmental disorder included in the autism spectrum disorders of the *Diagnostic and Statistical Manual*

Editor's Note: From Neihart, M. (2000). Gifted children with Asperger's Syndrome. *Gifted Child Quarterly*, 44(4), 222-230. © 2000 National Association for Gifted Children. Reprinted with permission.

DSM-IV) of the American Psychiatric Association (APA, 1994). Like other pervasive developmental disorders, it is characterized by serious impairment in social interaction skills and repetitive behaviors and is believed to be the result of a specific brain anomaly.

Since the 1980s, there has been increasing interest in pervasive developmental disorders. Individuals with these disorders share certain neuropsychological characteristics similar to autism, but do not meet the formal diagnostic criteria for autism. Asperger's Syndrome (AS) is one such variation (Atwood, 1998; Gillberg, 1992). Children with AS share a number of characteristics with gifted children. It can be challenging to determine whether a child's unusual development is a result of giftedness, a learning disability, or AS, especially among highly gifted children.

AS was first described in 1944 by Austrian physician Hans Asperger. He considered it to be a personality disorder characterized by pedantic speech content, impairment of two-way interactions, excellent logical abstract thinking, isolated areas of interest, repetitive and stereotyped play, and ignorance of environmental demands. AS individuals were thought to be capable of originality and creativity in selective fields (Tsai, 1992). Asperger (1979) suggested that his syndrome was more likely to be observed in children of high intelligence and special abilities. However, to date, the clinical literature on AS has focused on children with average or low-average intelligence. There has been surprisingly little examination of AS among gifted children (Barber, 1996; Cash, 1999a, 1999b).

Putting the Research to Use

Unlike autistic children who often receive special assistance in schools, the bright student with Asperger's Syndrome (AS) may be left to manage the best he or she can. In some cases, gifted students with the disorder may not be allowed to participate in their school's gifted program because teachers do not know how to make the necessary accommodations.

Experienced interdisciplinary teams can make an accurate diagnosis of AS when they include a developmental history and when they understand the reasons for a child's behaviors. Diagnostic evaluations include some formal testing, an assessment of motor skills, and observations of the child's social reciprocity and use of language.

Although no controlled studies have been conducted to empirically determine behaviors that distinguish gifted children with AS from other kinds of gifted children clinical observation and studies of gifted children and Asperger children suggest that distinctions may be made by examining their pragmatic use of language, their insight and ability to take others' perspective, the quality of their humor, their affective expression, and their response to disruptions of routine.

Effective teachers of gifted AS children understand that these students think very differently from other gifted children. To be successful in school, AS students often benefit from visual supports in order to manage the day-to-day routines and social demands of the classroom. Sensory integration therapy can be beneficial to gifted AS children whose hypersensitivity interferes with their learning or social adjustment. AS students can learn social skills with the aide of social stories, comic strip conversations, and other concrete, visual approaches.

In the past few years, there has been a growing recognition among clinicians and teachers that gifted children with AS are sometimes not diagnosed because their unusual behaviors are attributed to either their giftedness or to a learning disability. The purpose of this article is to discuss the similarities in developmental traits of AS children and gifted children and to suggest guidelines for distinguishing AS features among the gifted. In addition, this article suggests approaches for working with gifted children with AS.

ASPERGER CHILDREN

Information on the prevalence of AS is limited, but the disorder is more common in boys than in girls (APA, 1994). Clinical descriptions of AS children include the following characteristics: little to no empathy, monotonous speech patterns, highly idiosyncratic and intense interests (e.g., tide tables, a specified cartoon character, maps), social isolation as a result of inappropriate social communication, and inflexible thoughts and habits (Atwood, 1998; Barron & Barron, 1992; Grandin, 1992; Sacks, 1995). AS children are similar to children with other autism spectrum disorders in that they have problems with social communication and persistent idiosyncratic interests. Unlike many autistic children, however, AS children do not evidence delayed speech, the onset of their difficulties is somewhat later, and they more commonly experience motor deficits (Atwood, 1998; Frith, 1991; Grandin, 1992; Klin, 1994; Schopler & Mesibov, 1992; Szatmari, Bartolucci, & Bremner, 1989).

In contrast to children diagnosed with autism, AS children speak before age 5; do not remain aloof and withdrawn, but express some interest in people as they get older; are of at least average intelligence; and may show dramatic improvement as they grow older. As adults, AS children can become well-adapted and even very successful. They do tend to remain socially isolated, egocentric, and idiosyncratic. They often have difficulty working with others and have odd speech; they cannot do small talk and may seem fanatically or obsessively interested in limited topics. The eye contact of AS children is often odd. They may seem to gaze off or stare straight through those with whom they are conversing.

Others usually consider them "strange" or "weird" (Atwood, 1998; Barron & Barron, 1992; Grandin, 1992; Schopler & Mesibov, 1992; Szatmari, Bartolucci, Bremner, Bond, & Rich, 1989; Tantum, 1988).

Even within the subcategory of AS there is considerable variation. For instance, some perform poorly in school, while others achieve at a high level. Some have serious behavior problems, others do not. Some AS individuals demonstrate unacceptable habits, such as eating odd things, inappropriate touching, gnashing their teeth, and aggressive actions.

SIMILARITIES BETWEEN ASPERGER CHILDREN AND GIFTED CHILDREN

There seem to be at least seven characteristics common to gifted children and to children with AS. These commonalities have not been verified in any controlled studies, but are pulled from the shared literature and clinical experience. For instance, verbal fluency or precocity is common to both, and both may have excellent memories (Clark, 1992; Frith, 1991; Levy, 1988; Silverman, 1993). Both may evidence a fascination with letters or numbers and enjoy memorizing factual information at an early age. Both may demonstrate an absorbing interest in a specialized topic and may acquire vast amounts of factual information about it (Clark, 1992; Gallagher, 1985; Klin & Volkmar, 1995). They may annoy peers with their limitless talk about their interests. They may ask endless questions or give such lengthy and elaborately specific responses to questions that it seems they are unable to stop. One gifted AS child known to the author, when asked who Christopher Columbus was, responded with a dozen sentences detailing his genealogy.

Hypersensitivity to sensory stimuli is also not uncommon in both groups of children. Parents of gifted and AS children alike often can tell stories of their child's adamant refusal to wear certain kinds of materials, to eat foods of a certain texture, to recoil or run at the sound of noises they find particularly abrasive, or to refuse some kinds of touch.

AS children are described as having quite a range of abilities, as are gifted children. It was Asperger's observation that all children with the disorder seem to have "a special interest which enables them to achieve quite extraordinary levels of performance in a certain area" (p. 45). This interest is similar to the way in which gifted children are said to have "passions" (Betts & Kercher, 1999; Torrance, 1965). While they may demonstrate extraordinary skill in selected areas, both AS children and gifted children may perform in the average range in other areas (Baum, Owen, & Dixon, 1991; Wing, 1991). Both the gifted and the AS child are described as experiencing uneven development, particularly when cognitive development is compared to social and affective development at a young age (Altman, 1983; Asperger, 1991; Hollingworth, 1942; Silverman, 1993).

Table 1   Proposed Characteristics to Differentiate Ordinary Gifted Children from Gifted Children with Asperger's Syndrome

Differentiating Characteristic	Ordinary Gifted	Gifted with Asperger's Syndrome
Speech Patterns	Normal, but may have language of older child	Pedantic, seamless speech
Response to Routines	May passively resist, but will often go along	Very low tolerance for change, agitation, aggression
Awareness of Differences	Know they're different	Poor awareness of how others see them
Disturbance of Attention	If disturbance exists, it is usually external	Disturbance is internal
Humor	Engages in socially reciprocal humor	Can do word play, but typically doesn't understand humor that requires social reciprocity
Motor Clumsiness	Not characteristic of most gifted children	50-90% of Asperger children manifest
Inappropriate Affect	Not a characteristic	Nearly always observed
Insight	Insight usually good	Usually remarkably absent
Stereotypy	Not a characteristic	May be present

DISTINGUISHING NORMAL GIFTEDNESS FROM ASPERGER'S SYNDROME

Several similarities between gifted children and children with AS have been noted. Some of the distinguishing criteria are listed in Table 1. One distinguishing characteristic may be found in speech patterns. AS children, like ordinary gifted children, can evidence fluent speech that seems characterized by original and analytic thinking. Although both groups of children can be highly verbal, AS children are typically pedantic, while normal gifted children are not. Frith (1991) suggested a distinction may be made by the *seamlessness* of the speech. AS individuals may demonstrate seamless mixtures of knowledge and personal accounts in their written or oral responses to questions. They run on and on, blending content, personal reflections, and autobiographical illustrations. They do so perhaps because they are not aware of the purpose of the questions.

A second difference lies in how they respond to routines or structure. Although both are sometimes described as resistant to routine at home or school, ordinary gifted children are not nearly as rigid about routines as some AS children are. Also, gifted children, as a rule, do not have the kinds of difficulties coping with change that AS children have. AS children can have great difficulty with the lockstep scheduling and routine of traditional classrooms, and they may refuse to cooperate with common learning tasks of school. Gifted children may express displeasure about routines and may passively resist them, but they are not as likely to panic or become aggressive as are AS children.

Although both the gifted and the Asperger learner may complain about schedules and procedures, the latter is more likely to become obsessive about it (Barron & Barron, 1992; Clark, 1992; Klin & Volkmar, 1995).

There is also a difference in the whimsical behaviors that characterize AS children and some gifted children. Margaret Dewey (1992) wrote of the differences between autistic eccentricity and "garden variety eccentricity." Her observations may be useful to those trying to draw a line between normal gifted behaviors and AS behaviors. She noted that the normal eccentric person is aware that others will regard his or her eccentric behaviors as odd, while the individual with AS is not aware. People with AS often have no sense that they have done anything out of the ordinary. This obliviousness to social conventions is a trademark of the disorder. Several writers trace this obliviousness to the lack of a "theory of mind" (Atwood, 1998).

Theory of mind is akin to metacognition; it refers to knowing what one knows and how one knows it, while simultaneously processing differences in others. Theory of mind also subsumes the ability to take perspective; to be aware of oneself and to take another's perspective at the same time. Children with AS have great difficulty understanding the perspective of others, which is what makes their social adjustment so challenging (Schopler & Mesibov, 1992; Wing, 1981; Wing & Gould, 1979).

The criterion of obliviousness may serve to distinguish gifted children with and without Asperger's above age 7 or 8. For example, AS children may demonstrate excellent selective memory for people or events. Similarly, gifted children may demonstrate superb memory for selected topics of special interest to them. A difference, though, is that children with AS will assume others understand their references and will not be aware that others may find their memory remarkable in any way. In contrast, ordinary gifted children understand that others probably do not share their knowledge of selected topics and that others are surprised by their keen memory (Dewey, 1992).

A fourth distinction between the ordinary gifted child and the AS child has to do with the "disturbance of active attention" (Asperger, 1991, p. 76). Gifted children can have attention difficulties; but, when they do, it is usually because they are distracted by external stimuli. AS individuals are prone to distraction, but it is distraction that comes from within. They attend much less to external stimuli and more to their inner world. This internal distraction usually impairs their school performance.

Quality of humor is a fifth distinction. Gifted children with AS may be creative with word play and may even excel in making puns, but they lack the social reciprocity that underlies most humor (Atwood, 1998; Grandin, 1992; Van Bourgondien & Mesibov, 1987). They don't laugh at things that are funny to most people, and they often don't get the joke. Gifted children, on the other hand, are not characterized by deficits in their ability to understand humor.

Affective expression is the sixth potentially distinguishing feature. Children with Asperger's tend to present as automatons to some degree (Atwood, 1998). Their emotional response is often not what one would expect. It might be flattened or restricted, or they may laugh, get mad, or become anxious inappropriately. Inappropriate affective expression is not a common characteristic of gifted children.

Perhaps the most pronounced feature to distinguish a gifted AS student is his or her remarkable lack of insight and awareness regarding the feelings, needs, and interests of other people. An AS child will talk interminably in a monotonous or pedantic tone about a favorite topic, unaware that the listener might not be interested, needs to leave, is bored, or wants to say something. AS children will also interrupt private conversations and enter or leave abruptly without concern for the wishes or needs of others. They seem oblivious to the simplest rules of social conduct, and repeated efforts to instruct them or remind them do not change these behaviors. A pronounced lack of social awareness is not a common characteristic of ordinary gifted children. It is this struggle to understand the simplest social guidelines that frequently makes active participation in secondary gifted programs such a challenge for gifted students with AS (Szatmari, Bartolucci, & Bremner, 1989; Tantam, 1988; Wing, 1992; Wing & Gould, 1979).

The difficulties of identifying gifted AS individuals are compounded by the variations found among AS children. Stereotypy, for example, is observed in some, but not all AS children. Twisting hands, opening and closing a book, rocking, knocking, and whirling are examples of stereotypy that are sometimes, though not always, observed in AS children. When stereotypy is observed in a gifted child, however, a diagnosis of AS or another pervasive developmental disorder may be warranted and merits further examination (APA, 1994).

IDENTIFYING GIFTED CHILDREN WITH ASPERGER'S SYNDROME

It is imperative that gifted children with AS be diagnosed so that they can effectively secure appropriate services. Parents and teachers may agree that "something is wrong," but not know what. Identifying these students only as gifted or learning disabled is not as effective and can contribute not only to misunderstandings about the true nature of the child's difficulties, but also to the formulation of an inappropriate educational plan (Barron & Barron, 1992; Dewey, 1991; Grandin, 1992; Klin & Volkmar, 1995; Levy, 1988; Minshew, 1992; Schopler, 1985).

To identify AS in gifted children, two things are needed: a thorough developmental history and insight into the motivation behind certain behaviors (Atwood, 1998; Levy, 1988; Tsai, 1992). Without these two, there is a danger that AS will be over—or under—diagnosed. Symptoms of the disorder in a gifted child may be mistakenly attributed to the child's giftedness, rather than to the disorder. At other times, an AS child's giftedness may be discounted or considered irrelevant to his or her development.

Accurate diagnosis of AS in gifted children requires the participation of an experienced, interdisciplinary team. Parents should be actively involved in the

Table 2   The American Psychiatric Association's (1994) Diagnostic Criteria
for 299.80 Asperger's Disorder

A. Qualitative impairment in social interaction, as manifested by at least two of the following:
1. marked impairment in the use of multiple nonverbal behaviors, such as eye-to-eye gaze, facial expression, body postures, and gestures to regulate social interaction;
2. failure to develop peer relationships appropriate to developmental level;
3. a lack of spontaneous seeking to share enjoyment, interests, or achievements with other people (e.g., by a lack of sharing, bringing, or pointing out objects of interest to other people); and
4. lack of social or emotional reciprocity.

B. Restricted repetitive and stereotyped patterns of behavior, interests, and activities, as manifested by at least one of the following:
1. encompassing preoccupation with one or more stereotyped and restricted patterns of interest that is abnormal either in intensity or focus;
2. apparently inflexible adherence to specific, nonfunctional routines or rituals;
3. stereotyped and repetitive motor mannerisms (e.g., hand or finger flapping or twisting, or complex whole-body movements); and
4. persistent preoccupation with parts of objects.

C. The disturbance causes clinically significant impairment in social, occupational, or other important areas of functioning.

D. There is no clinically significant delay or general delay in language (e.g., single words used by age 2, communicative phrases used by age 3).

E. There is no clinically significant delay in cognitive development or in the development of age-appropriate self-help skills, adaptive behavior (other than social interaction), curiosity about the environment in childhood.

F. Criteria are not met for another specific Pervasive Developmental Disorder or schizophrenia.

---

assessment since developmental history is so important to confirming or ruling out the diagnosis. Table 2 provides the diagnostic criteria for AS from the *Diagnostic and Statistical Manual of Mental Disorders* (DSM-IV; APA, 1994).

Tony Atwood (1998) explained that, in addition to the developmental history, a diagnostic evaluation will usually include some formal testing, an assessment of movement skills, observations of the child's social reciprocity in situations engineered to elicit a variety of specific behaviors, and observations of the child's pragmatic use of language. Readers interested in a more comprehensive discussion of diagnostic tools and procedures are referred to his work.

Unlike autistic children who often receive special assistance in schools, the bright AS student may be left to manage the best he or she can. Relationships with teachers and peers can be extremely difficult. Over time, such children may become depressed as a result of their social isolation. Severe anxiety states can also be present. Until very recently, educators often did not know how to help the AS student, and some gifted students with the disorder were finding that they could not participate in their school's gifted program because no one knew how to make the necessary accommodations. Fortunately, great gains have been made in our knowledge in just the last few years, and we can now recommend specific instructional and behavior management strategies that should facilitate the inclusion of gifted children with AS (Atwood, 1998; Cumine, Leach, & Stevenson, 1997; Freeman & Dake, 1996; Gray, in press) Also, there are several research projects under way at this time that promise to yield yet more data about effective approaches for parenting and teaching the AS child.

WORKING WITH THE GIFTED ASPERGER'S STUDENT

AS children typically have difficulties in three areas: learning, socializing, and behaviors. Klin and Volkmar (1995) and Mesibov (1992) recommended that interventions focus on information, general support, and the management of specific problem behaviors. AS students can benefit by learning compensatory strategies, just as gifted students with learning disabilities do (Baum, Owen, & Dixon, 1991; Klin & Volkmar, 1995; Rourke, 1989). However, the way in which these strategies are taught must take into account the unique characteristics of an AS brain. People with AS are usually strong visual thinkers. They think best in concrete, literal pictures. This can have several advantages, but it is a distinct disadvantage in a classroom where the expectation is that the student think verbally. Frequent use of diagrams, visualization, and pictograms for teaching and managing behavior is widely recommended (Atwood, 1998; Grandin & Scariano, 1996; Gray, in press; Hurlburt, Frappe, & Frith, 1994).

Klin and Volkmar (1995) stressed that parts-to-whole verbal instruction is the most appropriate approach because AS children tend to overfocus on details. Care must be taken to teach strategies in the exact sequence students will need to use them to be successful. Unlike ordinary gifted children, rote styles of learning are recommended for AS children; they enjoy them because their own thoughts and habits are rigid.

Schopler and Mesibov (1992) suggested that a teacher with strong intuitive abilities is more likely to have success teaching a gifted AS child than is the teacher who bases decisions on logical deductions because AS students are often extremely sensitive to the tone with which something is said (Asperger, 1979; Frith, 1991). They respond not so much to what is said to them, but to how it is said. For this reason, it may be wise to keep directives or corrections short and to the point and avoid lengthier explanations that increase the chance that the child will distort the message.

[A]ll educational transactions have to be done with the affect "turned off." The teacher must never become angry nor should he aim to become loved. It will never do to appear quiet and calm on the outside while one is boiling inside. Yet this is only too likely, given the negativism and seemingly calculated naughtiness of autistic children! The teacher must at all cost be calm and collected and must remain in control. He should give his instructions in a cool and objective manner, without being intrusive. (Asperger, 1991, p. 48)

Sensory Integration

Extreme sensitivity to some kinds of sensory stimuli is common among children with AS (Tupper, 1999). Atwood (1998) stated that sound and touch are the most common sensitivities and that, for many of these children, "ordinary sensations are perceived as unbearably intense. The mere anticipation of the experience can lead to intense anxiety or panic" (p. 129). This hypersensitivity causes problems for the children in their adjustment to school.

For example, some AS students don't like the sound of the school bells, and others become aggressively oppositional when the teacher tries to coax them to join the class in an activity that involves touch. Those teaching gifted AS students would do well to respect these sensitivities and work with parents and therapists to teach AS students coping strategies. Some sensory stimuli can be avoided or minimized, but much of it cannot. Wearing silicone earplugs when needed or a headset with music may be enough of a sound barrier to assist some students. Others could benefit from sensory integration therapy to reduce their tactile defensiveness.

Sensory integration is a concept originally developed by Jean Ayres (1979), and it refers to the neurological process of taking in sensory information from the world, combining it with internal sensory information, and making adaptive responses to the environment. Adaptive responses are an essential component of getting through life. Tupper (1999) explained that the world is a constantly changing place to which most people respond spontaneously without thinking much and without a lot of stress. But, for people who misinterpret sensory information or who interpret sensory information slowly, the world is a much less predictable place and, therefore, much more frightening. They lack the means to respond easily. The more severe the sensory integration problem, the less tolerance a person has for stress and change. The individual may withdraw from or aggressively resist situations to keep from becoming overwhelmed. Since we are limited in how predictable we can make the world, we must work to increase their range of reactions—their flexibility. The aim of sensory integration therapy is to move people toward a wider repertoire of skills, "a more organized approach to the world" (Tupper, 1999).

Sensory integration therapy is designed to improve integration and reduce sensory sensitivity; it helps people organize, concentrate, attend, and anticipate and prepare for change. It can significantly increase a child's adaptability and flexibility, thus facilitating his or her greater participation in educational programs. It is now believed that there is no age limit on receiving benefits from such therapy, though younger children typically show greater improvement (Ayres, 1979; Tupper, 1999).

Sensory integration therapy is designed by specially trained occupational therapists. It provides sensory experiences that target deficit areas. The goal of sensory integration therapy is to nudge along the development of targeted sensory systems. Some of the exercises can be easily taught to school personnel and parents so that the child can receive the benefits at school and at home. For instance, deep pressure stimulation like joint compressions or hand massage can be provided at school as needed to help the AS child from becoming overstimulated, anxious, or aggressive. Rubbing or brushing exercises are also helpful for some children. Teachers should consult with the occupational therapist in their district regarding the application of these tools for particular students.

Social Skills Training

There is evidence that the AS child's problems with socialization can be improved by social training. However, concrete visual approaches must be used (Atwood, 1998; Mesibov, 1992). Talking about appropriate behaviors is not effective. Working with a mirror and imitative exercises can help (Klin & Volkmar, 1995), and Grandin (1992) suggested videotaping to teach new behaviors.

Carol Gray's Social Stories and comic strip conversations (Atwood, 1998; Gray, in press) are widely used to help children with all kinds of autism spectrum disorders develop social understanding. Social Stories is a technique to teach the cues and behaviors for specific social situations. It also helps teachers to understand the student's perspective and the reasons behind eccentric or idiosyncratic behaviors. The technique involves writing a very short story that describes a specific social situation with which the child struggles. The stories include four types of sentences: descriptive, perspective, directive, and control. Descriptive sentences explain where, who, and what. Perspective sentences explain the feelings and behaviors of others in the situation. Directives are statements about what the child is expected to do or say. The story concludes with a control sentence that is a statement about strategies the child can use to remember or understand the expected behavior in the social situation. Gray recommends a ratio of one directive and/or control sentence for every 2 to 5 descriptive and/or perspective sentences. The following is an example of a social story written for an AS child who is trying to understand popular figures of speech:

> Sometimes my friend, Toni, tells me to "chill" [descriptive]. This means I am getting loud and bossy [descriptive]. Toni doesn't want to sit with me when I am loud and bossy [perspective]. I will lower my voice when Toni tells me to "chill" [directive]. When Toni says "chill," I can imagine putting my voice on ice [control].

These students can be aided by some education about emotionality and by explanations about the perspectives of others. Education that includes validating and clarifying what is typical for people with AS can reduce anxiety and promote self-understanding. If there is trust with adults, the child is more likely to accept feedback (Klin & Volkmar, 1995). Mesibov (1992) recommended taking an active, directive, and structured approach.

Behavior Problems

Children with AS usually have some behavior problems. They may be compulsive or hyperactive. They may be prone to tantrums or aggressive outbursts. They may routinely hit other children without provocation or touch people in inappropriate ways. Some AS children suffer from anxiety attacks or specific phobias. They may be sensitive to teasing, but consistently demonstrate provocative behaviors that invite teasing. Some AS children will engage adults in endless arguments if given the opportunity. Parents especially may find themselves trapped in repeated discussions about the same events or disagreements. Adults should not attempt to reason for more than a minute with such children (Barton & Barron, 1992; Dewey, 1991; Klin & Volkmar, 1995). Brief, concrete directives are most effective. Visual supports like pictograms can be posted on a child's notebook, desk, or on the wall to visually cue the child regarding expected behaviors. The addition of visual supports can be remarkably effective in helping AS students organize their behavior. Teachers and parents should consult with an augmentative communication specialist to learn more about visual supports.

In addition to behavioral and educational approaches, medications may be helpful in treating specific problematic behaviors. Medications can significantly improve the quality of life of AS children when they exhibit compulsive or aggressive behaviors that interfere with school adjustment or family life. Medication may also be needed to alleviate symptoms of depression, thought disorder, or anxiety attacks. Tofranil and Prozac have been recommended (Grandin, 1992). Beta blockers have been helpful for some aggressive AS children, and Anafranil, Luvox, or one of the SSRIs (e.g., Zoloft) can be useful in reducing obsessive-compulsive tendencies (Gragg & Francis, 1997; Rapoport, 1989).

CONCLUSION

Parents and educators may attribute the difficulties gifted AS students have in school to a poor match between the curriculum or pedagogy and the child's learning needs. They may mistakenly put all the focus on the child's giftedness and fail to identify AS. In addition, the social deficits of some gifted children may be attributed to their giftedness or to a learning disability when a diagnosis of AS would be more appropriate. The school is sometimes blamed for not understanding and accommodating the unique needs of the gifted learner when, in fact, the problem is that the child's disorder has not been identified or addressed.

Accurate diagnosis is necessary to obtain appropriate assistance. The social skills training that benefits AS children is different from the social skills training that benefits children with other kinds of learning problems (Guevremont, 1990; Klin & Volkmar, 1995; Mesibov, 1992; Wing, 1992). Accurate diagnosis increases the chance that students will receive appropriate services and have maximum opportunity to realize their potential.

There has been tremendous interest and a surge of research and publications about AS in the last five years, but giftedness is rarely mentioned (Cash, 1999a, 1999b). Fortunately, there are studies under way that will improve our understanding of gifted children with the disorder (Henderson, 1999). Many excellent resources are available online and in print for educators and parents who want more information about how to effectively teach the child with AS. Barbara Kirby's website (http://www.udel.edu.bkirby/asperger.html) and the Yale Child Study Center's website (http://www.info.med.yale.edu/chldstdy/autism.html) are two comprehensive sites. Kirby's site includes sample IEP goals, forms, and checklists to be used with AS students.

ASPEN (Asperger's Syndrome Education Network) is a national organization recently formed to provide support and information to individuals with neurological disorders like Asperger's, High Functioning Autism, and Pervasive Developmental Disorder Not Otherwise Specified. They provide a helpline at (904) 745-6741, and they publish a quarterly newsletter for members. Their excellent website http://www.asperger.org) provides an annotated list of the latest publications about the disorder, as well as helpful links to other sites.

Able autistic individuals can rise to eminent positions and perform with such outstanding success that one may even conclude that only such people are capable of certain achievements. It is as if they had compensatory abilities to counterbalance their deficiencies. Their unswerving determination and penetrating intellectual powers, part of their spontaneous and original mental activity, their narrowness and single-mindeness, as manifested in their special interests, can be immensely valuable and can lead to outstanding achievements in their chosen areas. We can see in the autistic person, far more clearly than with any normal child, a line of work often grows naturally out of their special abilities (Asperger, 1991, p. 88).

REFERENCES

Altman, R. (1983). Social-emotional development of gifted children and adolescents: A research model. *Roeper Review, 6*, 65–67.

American Psychiatric Association. (1994). *Diagnostic and statistical manual of mental disorders* (4th ed.). Washington, DC: Author.

Asperger, H. (1979). Problems of infantile autism. *Communication, 13*, 45–52.

Asperger, H. (1991). Autistic psychopathy in childhood. In U. Frith (Ed. and Trans.), *Autism and Asperger Syndrome* (pp. 37–92). London: Cambridge University Press.

Atwood, T. (1998). *Asperger's Syndrome: A guide for parents and professionals*. Philadelphia: Taylor and Francis.

Ayres, J. (1979). *Sensory integration and the child.* Los Angeles: Western Psychological Services.

Barber, C. (1996). The integration of a very able pupil with Asperger's Syndrome into a mainstream school. *British Journal of Special Education, 23,* 19–24.

Barron, J., & Barron, S. (1992). *There's a boy in here.* New York: Simon and Schuster.

Baum, S., Owen, S., & Dixon, J. (1991). *To be gifted and learning disabled: From identification to practical intervention strategies.* Mansfield, CT: Creative Learning Press.

Betts, G., & Kercher, J. (1999). *Autonomous learner model: Optimizing ability.* Greeley, CO: ALPS.

Cash, A. (1999a). A profile of gifted individuals with autism: The twice-exceptional learner. *Roeper Review, 22,* 22–27.

Cash, A. (1999b). Autism: The silent mask. In A. Y. Baldwin & W. Vialle (Eds.), *The many faces of giftedness* (pp. 209–238). Albany, NY: Wadsworth Publishing.

Clark, B. (1992). *Growing up gifted.* New York: Macmillan.

Cumine, V., Leach, J., & Stevenson, G. (1997). *Asperger Syndrome: A practical guide for teachers.* Philadelphia: Taylor and Francis.

Dewey, M. (1991). Living with Asperger's Syndrome. In U. Frith (Ed. and Trans.), *Autism and Asperger Syndrome* (pp. 184–206). London: Cambridge University Press.

Dewey, M. (1992). Autistic eccentricity. In E. Schopler & G. B. Mesibov (Eds.), *High functioning individuals with autism* (pp. 281–288). New York: Plenum Press.

Freeman, S., & Dake, L. (1996). *Teach me language: A language manual for children with autism, Asperger's Syndrome and related developmental disorders.* B.C. Canada: SKF Books.

Frith, U. (1991). Asperger and his syndrome. In U. Frith (Ed. and Trans.), *Autism and Asperger syndrome* (pp. 1–36). London: Cambridge University Press.

Gallagher, J. (1985). *Educating the gifted child.* Newton, MA: Allyn and Bacon.

Gillberg, C. (1992). Autism and autistic-like conditions: Subclasses among disorders of empathy. *Journal of Child Psychology and Psychiatry and Allied Disciplines, 33,* 813–842.

Gragg, R. A., & Francis, G. (1997). *Assessment and treatment of childhood obsessive-compulsive disorder.* Workshop presented at the 105th annual meeting of the American Psychological Association, Chicago, IL.

Grandin, T. (1992). An inside view of autism. In E. Schopler & G. B. Mesibov (Eds.), *High functioning individuals with autism* (pp. 105–128). New York: Plenum Press.

Grandin, T., & Scariano, M. (1996). *Emergence: Labeled autistic.* New York: Warner Books.

Gray, C. (in press). Social stories and comic strip conversations with students with Asperger Syndrome and high functioning autism. In E. Schopler, G. B. Mesibov, & L. Kunce (Eds.), *Asperger's Syndrome and high functioning autism.* New York: Plenum Press.

Guevremont, D. (1990). Social skills and peer relationship training. In R. Barkley (Ed.), *Attention deficit hyperactivity disorder: A handbook for diagnosis and treatment* (pp. 540–572). New York: The Guilford Press.

Henderson, L. (1999, December). *Gifted individuals with Asperger Syndrome.* Workshop presented at the annual convention of the Texas Association for the Gifted and Talented, Houston, TX.

Hollingworth, L. S. (1942). *Children above 180 IQ Stanford-Binet: Origin and development.* Yonkers-on-Hudson, NY: World Book.

Hurlburt, R. T., Frappe, F., & Frith, U. (1994). Sampling the form of inner experience of three adults with Asperger's Syndrome. *Psychological Medicine, 24,* 385–395.

Klin, A. (1994). Asperger Syndrome. *Child and Adolescent Psychiatry Clinic of North America, 3,* 131–148.

Klin, A., & Volkmar, F. R. (1995). *Guidelines for parents: Assessment, diagnosis, and intervention of Asperger Syndrome.* Pittsburgh, PA: Learning Disabilities Association of America.

Levy, S. (1988*). Identifying high-functioning children with autism.* Bloomington, IN: Indiana Resource Center for Autism.

Mesibov, G. (1992). Treatment issues with high-functioning adolescents and adults with autism. In E. Schopler & G. B. Mesibov (Eds.), *High functioning individuals with autism* (pp. 143–155). New York: Plenum Press.

Minshew, N. J. (1992). Neurological localization in autism. In E. Schopler & G. B. Mesibov (Eds.), *High functioning individuals with autism* (pp. 65–90). New York: Plenum Press.

Rapoport, J. (1989). *The boy who couldn't stop washing: The experiences and treatment of obsessive-compulsive disorder.* New York: E. P. Dutton.

Rourke, B. (1989). *Nonverbal learning disabilities: The syndrome and the model.* New York: Guilford Press.

Sacks, O. (1995). *An anthropologist on Mars.* New York: Vintage Books.

Schopler, E. (1985). Convergence of learning disability, higher level autism, and Asperger's Syndrome. *Journal of Autism and Developmental Disorders, 15,* 359.

Schopler, E., & Mesibov, G. B. (Eds.). (1992). *High-functioning individuals with autism.* New York: Plenum Press.

Silverman, L. K. (Ed.). (1993). *Counseling the gifted and talented.* Denver, CO: Love.

Szatmari, P., Bartolucci, G., & Bremner, R. (1989). Asperger's Syndrome: A review of clinical features. *Canadian Journal of Psychiatry, 34,* 554–560.

Szatmari, P., Bartolucci, G., Bremner, R., Bond, S., & Rich, S. (1989). A follow-up study of high functioning autistic children. *Journal of Autism and Developmental Disorders, 19,* 213–225.

Tantam, D. (1988). Lifelong eccentricity and social isolation: II. Asperger's Syndrome or schizoid personality disorder? *British Journal of Psychiatry, 153,* 783–791.

Torrance, P. (1965). *Gifted children in the classroom.* New York:. Macmillan.

Tsai, L. Y. (1992). Diagnostic issues in high-functioning autism. In E. Schopler & G. B. Mesibov (Eds.), *High functioning individuals with autism* (pp. 11–40). New York: Plenum Press.

Tupper, L. (1999, September). Sensory integration. Workshop presented at the Annual State Conference on Autism, Plano, TX.

Van Bourgondien, M. E., & Mesibov, G. B. (1987). Humor in high-functioning autistic adults. *Journal of Autism and Developmental Disorders, 17,* 417–424.

Wing, L. (1981). Asperger's Syndrome: A clinical account. *Psychological Medicine, 11,* 115–129.

Wing, L. (1991). The relationship between Asperger's Syndrome and Kanner's Autism. In U. Frith (Ed. and Trans.), *Autism and Asperger's Syndrome* (pp. 93–121). London: Cambridge University Press.

Wing, L. (1992). Manifestations of social problems in high-functioning autistic people. In E. Schopler & G. B. Mesibov (Eds.), *High functioning individuals with autism* (pp. 129–142). New York: Plenum Press.

Wing, L., & Gould, J. (1979). Severe impairments of social interaction and associated abnormalities in children: Epidemiology and classification. *Journal of Autism and Developmental Disorders, 9,* 11–29.

5

We Can't Change What We Don't Recognize: Understanding the Special Needs of Gifted Females

Sally M. Reis

The University of Connecticut

In this article, an overview of some of the major issues, questions and problems related to gifted females will be presented. These issues include the underachievement of gifted females; creative productivity of females; male dominance in mathematics and science; cultural stereotyping, sex roles and mixed message; lack of planning; the perfection complex and the imposter syndrome; concerns about counseling and special populations. Research related to the issues of ability, achievement, personality, social and environmental pressures related to gender will be briefly discussed and suggestions for future research directions will be made.

Editor's Note: From Reis, S. M. (1987). We can't change what we don't recognize: Understanding the special needs of gifted females. *Gifted Child Quarterly*, *31*(2), 83-89. © 1987 National Association for Gifted Children. Reprinted with permission.

In 1976, Heather, a sixth grade student who had spent seven months studying robotics and designing and building a life-sized robot as a part of her work in our gifted program, approached me with a disturbing observation. It seemed, she said, that the men and women who had been visiting our resource room had different comments and questions about her robot. Heather observed that the women who came to see the robot asked her about how she designed it, what kind of motor she had used, how she had gotten the idea, and other questions related to the process of building the robot. The men who visited, however, seemed to concentrate on asking one question in a rather teasing and playful way: Did you build the robot to do housework? At the time I was surprised by Heather's observation and thought she was mistaken in her conclusions. Yet, in the weeks that followed our conversation, I listened to the comments of those who visited our program and discovered that Heather's observation had been remarkably accurate. The first or second question that most male visitors, regardless of their age, asked about the robot concerned its ability to do housework. The question that we as educators and researchers must ask is: To what degree do the socialization and stereotypic experiences bright young girls have in their formative years impact upon their ability to fulfill their potential in their adult lives?

Few questions can be raised about whether or not the underachievement of bright women exists; the fact remains that in almost all professional fields and occupations, men overwhelmingly surpass women in both the professional accomplishments they achieve and the financial benefits they reap. Today, statistics show that women earn only 60% of men's wages and continue to receive only 60% as much Social Security benefits. It may be argued that these facts alone are not an adequate measurement of female underachievement; however, it is important to recognize that many gifted women look back at what they perceive as lost opportunities (Sears & Barbee, 1977; Goleman, 1980 a & b; White, 1984). If female underachievement is best measured by the many older women in our society who look back at their lives with feelings of regret and missed opportunities and say: "I might have but . . ." or "I could have if . . ." or "I never had time to . . .", it then becomes our responsibility to help future generations of females *before* it is too late.

In this article, an overview of some major issues, questions, and problems related to gifted females will be presented. Research related to the issues of ability, achievement, personality, social and environmental pressures, and gender will be discussed. After these issues are presented, suggestions will be made for new research to help females both recognize and realize their potential.

UNDERACHIEVEMENT OF GIFTED FEMALES

What is meant by underachievement of gifted females and at what age does it surface? The answer to these questions is important if we are to understand the disparity between male and female achievement and if our efforts to improve the situation are to be successful.

The definition of underachievement will vary with the age of the person being considered. For example, underachievement in young girls may best be described as failing to do as well as might be expected in school. Sex differences in underachievement have been found to first emerge in sixth grade or in junior or senior high school. According to Shaw and McCuen (1960), females differed from male underachievers who demonstrated a significant pattern of underachievement from first grade through high school. Fitzpatrick (1978) also found that the underachievement of females appears after puberty and that underachieving secondary students have grades that are equal or superior to those of later achievers in their elementary school years.

In more recent work, Stockard and Wood (1984) challenge what they term "... the myth of female underachievement..." (p. 825). In data gathered from students' cumulative secondary records (7–12th grades), they found that males were more likely than females to have total averages and grades in both English and mathematics that were lower than might be predicted by their scores on standardized tests of ability. However, since females receive higher grades than males throughout elementary school, high school, and college (Achenbach, 1970; Coleman, 1961; Davis, 1964), it might be argued that grades in school should not be equated with underachievement as has been suggested in these studies; for even though females receive higher grades throughout school, their adult professional productivity is lower. Stockard and Wood conclude from the results of their research, as well as other studies (Alexander & Ecklund, 1974, p. 679; Hauser, 1971, p. 110) "... that achievement, as measured by grades, must be seen as distinct from achievement measured by educational and occupational aspirations and attainment, and supports the contention that school achievement may well be perceived as an area where it is appropriate for females to excel..." (p. 835).

The underachievement of adult women, then, is a totally different concept than underachievement of younger women for it defies measurement by the grades one achieves in school. We might consider it in comparison with male standards of profession, status, career related accomplishments, satisfaction and productivity, or it may be that we have to reexamine the concept of underachievement of bright women who do not achieve similar professional accomplishments as their male counterparts. The realization of giftedness in women may need to be redefined to include the nurturance of one's children and family, the success of being an outstanding teacher or the joy of accomplishment from the pursuit of a career that still allows time for a satisfying personal life. However, every attempt must be made to help bright young females realize the myriad of choices and options available to them and to provide the advice and support they need to realize their potential in an area of their own choice. It then becomes our responsibility to work with bright young females and monitor their progress to watch for signs of underachievement in their school experiences. If they begin to consciously refrain from doing their best work because of fears of being rejected socially (Horner, 1972; Lavach & Lanier, 1975; Stockard, 1980), counseling and support from parents and teachers can help to change the situation before it is too late. We must keep in mind that underachievement of gifted females is often not reflected in grades or how well one "goes to school" but rather, in what a person believes can be attained or accomplished in life.

Creative Productivity of Females

"Men professors produce more creative work in the form of research publication and books than women professors" (Groth, 1975, p. 334). Callahan (1979) observed " . . . that girls earn higher grades in school, yet men write more books, earn more degrees, produce more works of art, and make more contributions in all professional fields" (p. 402). The lack of adult creative productivity in females has been noted in various research studies. Even in areas such as literature, where both sexes believe that females excel, men are more productive. A recent National Endowment for the Arts list of 100 recipients for Fellowships in Literature included only 30% women.

One of the major reasons that males are demonstrating more creative productivity may simply be that they have more time for their work and less home-related duties and outlets. Many extremely bright women who assume the primary responsibility for domestic chores or who are single parents demonstrate their own creativity in ways related to their family or home: in the Halloween costumes they design for their children, the way they decorate their homes, the meals they prepare, the errands they run, and even the clothes that they make. Because women still assume the primary responsibility as family nurturer and caretaker, many creative energies are directly channeled into the family and home while their spouse's creative energy is free to be directly applied to his work.

Women who work within or outside of the home, or who are married or single parents may simply not have the time to be creative producers. Some of the counseling techniques that are recommended for bright girls to encourage them to learn the techniques of being "Queen Bees" (Staines, Tavris, & Jayaratne, 1974) from adult mentors may need to be examined. The "Queen Bee Syndrome" describes a woman who is able to succeed like a male in work-related activities while simultaneously maintaining her femininity and succeeding as a mother and wife. A reexamination of those older role models may be necessary because many highly productive women classified as high achievers exist by putting out maximum energy at all times, trying to do everything and do it well. It is not enough that they attempt to be outstanding in their work; their perfection complex also causes them to strive for a Jane Fonda body, a house that could be on the cover of *Better Homes and Gardens,* and perfect children. They wear themselves out trying to do everything well, often with minimal help from their spouses, and yet still feel plagued by guilt that they may not have given their husbands, children, home, and career enough time, care, and attention.

The answer to this dilemma, of course, lies in the education of men to assume an equal partnership in a relationship to enable women to be freed from some of their responsibilities and given the same kind of opportunities as men have. Until this occurs, however, teaching young gifted females to be Queen Bees may be a disservice to them. Instead, we may be better off to teach them that it is impossible to be perfect in everything we do so that we may not be able to do everything well, and that choices about careers, marriage, and children will have to be made.

Male Dominance in Mathematics and Science

When Barbara McClintock won the Nobel Prize for Science in 1983, she was only the fifth woman to receive this award in the 80 years since it was established (Dembart, 1984). According to recent statistics compiled by the National Science Foundation, the number of women and minorities pursuing scientific careers has increased in the last fifteen years. Between 1972 and 1982, the number of women scientists and engineers increased 200%. However, of the nearly 2 million American engineers, only 3.5% are women and of the 225,000 physical scientists, only 12% are women (Dembart, 1984). Similar trends are apparent in mathematics. Research about the decline in both mathematic and scientific ability of females has been well reported and has caused considerable controversy (Fennema, 1974; Fennema & Sherman, 1977; MacCoby & Jacklin, 1974). Most notable is the attention given to an article (Benbow & Stanley, 1980) which attributes higher math scores of boys to endogenous variables rather than social factors. The controversy that has erupted from that article has produced both speculation and further research. Pallas and Alexander (1983) have suggested that females need to be encouraged to pursue advanced course work in math and science in high school in order to overcome their deficiencies. Concerns about the advice young women receive from guidance counselors, parents, and teachers have been noted in previous articles related to gifted females (Callahan, 1979; Casserly, 1975; Fitzgerald & Crites, 1980). The Benbow and Stanley research may lead some counselors and teachers to conclude that females are inferior in mathematics and science. The following letter from a parent emphasizes an attitude problem that may be more prevalent in our country than any of us realize:

> My daughter, an honors student who was later admitted to the biology honors program at The University of Connecticut, was experiencing difficulty in an Honors Physics class of 10 students. Only two girls were in the class and when I contacted her teacher (a male), he threw up his hands and told me that girls were never good at physics! I wonder if part of the problem might have been his attitude and lack of understanding?
>
> O'Keefe, D., Personal Communication
>
> July 25, 1985.

There are still no definitive answers to the question of why men outperform women in mathematics and science. Thus, a proper concern for equity dictates maximum efforts be made to help men and women (boy and girls also) achieve to the highest levels possible.

FACTORS CONTRIBUTING TO UNDERACHIEVEMENT

Cultural Stereotyping, Sex Roles, and Mixed Messages

Sexual stereotyping regarding females exists throughout our society; one need only glance at a magazine, turn on a television, or read some popular children's books to be reminded of the differences in cultural expectations for males and females. The September 1985 edition of *Psychology Today*, for example, features an advertisement on the back cover depicting a man using a telescope (caption . . . he likes the planets) and a woman reading a book about Hollywood (caption . . . she likes the stars). This stereotyping delivers powerful messages to bright young females about their role in life, their own importance, and their worth as a person (Callahan, 1979; Pogrebin, 1980; Schwartz, 1980). Bright young girls are often caught in a bind between their intelligence and their sex (Rodenstein, Pfleger, & Colangelo, 1977; Schwartz, 1980). For example, an eager, questioning mind may cause a bright student to call out in class, to debate, to argue, to ask questions. A young boy who does this may be labeled precocious while a bright young girl who asks too many questions may be labeled obnoxious, aggressive, or even unfeminine.

In a recent study, Myra and David Sadker (1985) found that boys vocally dominate the classroom. In more than a hundred fourth, fifth, and sixth grade classes in four states and the District of Columbia, they found that boys get more attention and encouragement than do girls. "We found that at all grade levels, in all communities, and in all subject areas, boys dominated classroom communication" (pp. 54, 56). The Sadker research also demonstrated that teachers behaved differently when boys or girls called out in class without raising their hand. When boys answered without being called on, teachers accepted their answers; the same behavior from girls, however, resulted in negative responses about raising their hands. The Sadkers believe that their research indicates a subtle but powerful message for girls: "Boys should be academically assertive and grab teacher attention; girls should act like ladies and keep quiet" (p. 56). Being eager and assertive in the questions that one may want to ask in school may also contrast sharply with the polite manners parents expect from their daughters. This confusion about appropriate behavior and the mixed messages received from parents and peers is best described in a letter written by a nineteen-year-old female who attended a workshop on the problems faced by gifted females:

Caught in the double-bind of being labeled gifted, being told I can do anything, being treasured as a bright young person, and at the same time being told not to compete, not to try to "run with the guys," not to show off, to "be a lady," I spent many years and much invaluable energy in the psychic bind of the gifted girl. Even now, although the circumstances have changed (after all, I *am* in college!), I still fight the same old battles of outside expectations, awkward roles, and self-sabotage. Just seeing that there are actually people thinking about these issues was enormously supportive for me, and here, too, I thank you for the doors you opened.

Brush, L., Personal Communication

September 2, 1982.

Current research indicates that girls are treated differently in classrooms in college as well as elementary and secondary school (Schmidt, 1982). Bright females with many questions and ideas suffer perhaps more than any other group in the mixed messages they receive from their parents, teachers, and peers. Counseling for parents and students and the support that may be received in gifted programs may help to alleviate these mixed messages (Bardwick, 1972; Callahan, 1979; Rodenstein, Pfleger, & Colangelo, 1977; Stein & Bailey, 1973).

Fear of Success

The fear of success syndrome first introduced by Horner (1972), is believed by many researchers to be another key factor in understanding the problems facing bright women. Fear of success may cause some females to believe that they may be rejected by their peers or appear undesirable to the opposite sex if they are too competent or successful (Horner, 1972; Lavach & Lanier, 1975). Counseling work with adolescent gifted females has demonstrated that some do hold back from answering in class for fear that their peers and prospective boyfriends may think that they are "too smart." Fear of success may lead to a change in confidence in one's ability that can have devastating effects if it occurs during college or graduate school. Although more current research suggests that fear of success can be eliminated with age and experience (Birnbaum, 1975; Hoffman, 1977) preliminary findings in a study of high school valedictorians found that female students, who had done well in high school, lose confidence in their ability after a few years of college (Arnold & Denny, 1985). The effects of this loss of self-confidence can influence the rest of a young woman's life if it causes changes in college plans or goals for graduate study.

Lack of Planning

Another issue that has emerged in counseling and has been reported in the literature (Wolleat, 1979) is the inability of many bright young females to plan for the future in a realistic way. Many bright young females ignore or are unaware of the economic realities of womens' lives and the fact that most of them will have to work their entire lives to support themselves and/or their families. Many young females believe that someone will come along who will take care of them and support them and consequently never even consider long-term planning for a career or the financial implications of their choices. Males, on the other hand, grow up realizing that they must plan for a lifetime career and, accordingly, make better choices and select more appropriate long range goals. Because women do not learn to plan, they often have not thought about how they can juggle a marriage, a career, family, and/or graduate school. Some bright young women have totally unrealistic views of how they can go through college, graduate school, and then interrupt their career to be married and have children without realizing what this can do to chances of advancement in their professional lives. Could a bright young male executive interrupt his newly developing career for seven or eight years without serious ramifications? Females need to be aware of these consequences and encouraged at an early age through counseling to begin planning their education and considering careers will allow them to flourish both professionally and personally.

The Perfection Complex and the Imposter Syndrome

In working with gifted young females during the last ten years, some issues have emerged that seem to be factors in the realization of potential. One issue related to the problems faced by gifted females is a personality trait that might be labeled the "perfection complex." Many bright young females believe that they must be perfect in everything they attempt to do. Accordingly, they invest considerable energy in trying to be the best athlete, the best dancer, the best scholar, the best friend, and the best daughter. Additionally, bright young girls often feel that they must also be slender, beautiful, and popular. The perfection complex causes them to set unreasonable goals for themselves and to constantly strive to achieve at ever higher levels. The fascinating anomaly of this perfection complex occurs when high levels of success have been achieved by females and has been labeled "the Great Imposter Syndrome" (Clance, 1985; Machlowitz, 1982; Warschaw, 1985). This syndrome describes what may be interpreted as an extremely low sense of self-esteem and occurs when females attribute their success to factors other than their own efforts and see their outward image as a bright successful achiever as being undeserved or accidental. "I was lucky, I was in the right place at the right time, I really didn't do as well as it seems, I had a lot of help" are all statements that females may make when they are complimented on their success. This reaction to success does not seem to affect males to the same degree. In short, bright young males seem to attribute their achievements to their own efforts, while girls attribute their accomplishments to external forces and not to themselves (Parsons, Ruble, Hodges, & Small, 1976; Deaux & Emswiller, 1974).

Concerns About Counseling

The last issue related to bright young women that should be considered by those who work in the field of gifted education is the kind of counseling used to encourage them to pursue advanced course work, graduate school, and fulfilling professional lives. Without making any value judgments, we must realize that a demanding professional career will undoubtedly result in choices having to be made. As Carol Gilligan so sensitively points out in her book, *In a Different Voice* (1982), the value systems of women are different. If, as Gilligan believes, women view moral concerns in terms of interpersonal relationships and responsibilities to others, they may have a difficult, if not impossible, time putting their own needs in front of the needs of those they care about. The different voice that Gilligan discusses lies in an ethic of caring and a tie between relationship and responsibility.

Gilligan's cogent observations should have an impact on anyone doing counseling work with bright young women. Until men begin to assume a partnership approach to relationships, encouraging young females to pursue demanding careers may, to some extent, discourage them from marriage and motherhood or cause them to feel constantly guilty about their work and its effect on their home life. Any counseling work should include a discussion of options and a consideration of balance; young women should be encouraged to think about what is important to them and to realize that a possibility exists for combining what they value with a meaningful career. At the same time, they should also realize that it may not be possible to combine some professional careers with a happy marriage, the raising of children, and the care of a home and family. If the ethic of caring that Gilligan describes is so important to women, the way we view female "giftedness" may have to be expanded beyond an assessment of womens' professional accomplishments.

SPECIAL POPULATIONS

Underlying the problem of achievement of gifted females are certain cultural and environmental factors that are overwhelming influences in their lives. Without a doubt, these cultural and environmental influences can be positive; women who complete a doctorate are more apt to come from higher socioeconomic homes and have professional or successful executive parents (Anastasi & Schaefer, 1969; Astin, Suniewick, & Dweck, 1974; Gysbers, Johnston, Gust, 1975; as cited in Groth, 1975). Higher socioeconomic status may not only result in financial capacity to send a daughter to college and graduate school, but also in the encouragement, expectation, and counseling that parents provide to help their daughters gain the independence and self-confidence necessary to leave home and attend college. This encouragement and counseling may be less prevalent in lower socioeconomic families where parents do not have the experience of having attended college themselves or the knowledge to help their daughters examine scholarship opportunities or loan applications.

We cannot measure the lost potential of gifted females without calling special attention to the problems of disadvantaged, minority females. How many Black, Native American, or Hispanic girls have the potential to become scientists, writers, artists, or musicians, but will not because they never believe it to be within their reach? We must acknowledge that escaping poverty and ignorance to meet one's potential is difficult enough for males who expect to have a lifetime of work. Females who are expected to care for brothers and sisters, cook the family's meals, keep the house clean, marry young and have children of their own, may lose the opportunity for a different future. Therefore, intervention and counseling strategies should be provided for minority, disadvantaged, and special population gifted females at an early age to help them explore their options and make a choice that will reflect their interests and talents.

CURRENT RESEARCH AND FUTURE RESEARCH DIRECTIONS

Although research related to gifted females is more prevalent than it was a decade ago, it is certainly not being carried on to the degree that it might. As Callahan (1979) has stated, "Underlying the problems of achievement and motivation of gifted and talented females lie hypotheses yet to be tested and perhaps untestable in the experimental tradition" (p. 412). A major concern related to research in the area is lack of control over the environmental and societal factors that influence young girls. "Until cultural or environmental factors are altered considerably to neutralize the potential effects, there will be no way of asserting how great that impact is" (p. 412). Since we will not be able to radically change the cultural or environmental factors in our society within the next few years, research related to gifted females should be concentrated in three areas.

The first area is the identification of the degree that cultural, societal, and environmental factors impact upon the educational experiences of students and how the impact, if negative, can be controlled. For example, the Sadker (1985) research on sexism in schools in the 80's included a treatment involving sixty teachers from the study who received four days of training to establish equity in classroom interactions. The Sadkers found that teachers who received the training succeeded in eliminating classroom bias as well as improving overall teaching effectiveness, and enabling teachers to initiate a higher level of intellectual discussion. A similar type of research questioned the socialization explanations for sex differences in mathematical performance (Pallas & Alexander, 1983) and found that SAT math performance differs considerably when sex differences in quantative high school coursework are controlled. The Pallas and Alexander research suggests that increasing females' enrollment in advanced math courses would reduce differences in SAT math performance. Since this research suggests that experience and socialization have an impact upon performance, it also clarifies the need for research in which these factors can be controlled by the school experiences we provide.

The second area of research currently being considered relates to the internal barriers experienced by females that might have an impact on their ability to realize their potential. These personality and socialization factors include: self-esteem, efficacy, locus of control, fear of success, underachievement, and others. Research of this type has been conducted by Hollinger and Fleming (1984), who studied the effects of the internal barriers of underachievement, non-assertiveness, fear of success, social competence, and self-esteem on the realization of potential, and Kramer (1985) who studied the effects of social interactions and perception of ability. In both of these studies, no treatment was offered to assist the subjects in overcoming their internal barriers. If a counselling program had been initiated, successful female role models introduced, and teacher/counselor/parent training provided, results of the post-treatment analysis might have yielded different findings. One problem with research on high school age females which is not longitudinal is that differences in motivation, fear of success, and other personality variables, may not surface until college years.

The third type of research relates to longitudinal/developmental studies of both females and males. This type of research is, of course, influenced by the societal changes that may result in the emergence of a culture that differs from the beginning to the ending years of the study. Longitudinal research can provide valuable information related to the time in life at which various blocks to achievement occur.

Future efforts in research should concentrate on treatments that can alleviate the problems that have been identified by prior research. In order to provide a gauge by which we can measure the impact of the women's movement and history upon societal changes, research on the different social and emotional development of gifted females and males should continue. For example, a recent study (Leroux, 1985) conducted with 60 grade twelve students in Ontario found differences in learning, social interactions, career aspiration, and self-image between gifted males and females. This research also indicates that females still believe males are more capable in mathematics and science, and males perceive females as more capable in English and literature. This points to the need for even more counseling in this area.

Longitudinal research is also needed on the effect of single-sex advanced math and science classes coupled with counseling and the presence of female role models over a prolonged period of time. If, as Fox (1977) has determined, young girls do better in math if they have a female teacher and are in predominately female classes, we need to examine what effects an early and prolonged program of that kind might have on both the ability scores and the pursuit of scientific and mathematical careers. This type of intervention might also be extremely beneficial for minority or disadvantaged females.

Qualitative research relating to the attributes of women who have achieved is also needed. If we can identify the personality and societal factors that enabled women to become successful, we can share this information with parents and *educators and provide the advice, guidance,* and insights needed for young females to successfully embark upon their road to self-fulfillment.

No doubt exists that research on the abilities of females has made progress from the Victorian age, when scientists argued that if women used their brains excessively, they would impair their fertility by draining off blood cells needed to support their menstrual cycle (Newsweek, 1981). However, until young women have the same opportunities to grow, flourish, and achieve without the sexual stereotypes and negative influences reported in the literature, more research must be conducted to determine how we can make schools, homes, and society in general, more sympathetic to and supportive of the special problems faced by gifted females.

REFERENCES

Achenbach, T. M. (1970). Standardization of a research instrument for identifying associative responding in children. *Developmental Psychology, 2,* 283–291.

Alexander, K. L., & Ecklund, B. K. (1974). Sex differences in the educational attainment process. *American Sociological Review, 39,* 668–682.

Anastasi, A., & Schaefer, C. (1969). Biographical correlates of artistic and literary creativity in adolescent girls. *Journal of Applied Psychology, 53*(4), 267–278.

Astin, H., Suniewick, N., & Dweck, S. (1974). *Women: A bibliography on their education and careers.* New York: Behavioral Publications, Inc.

Bardwick, J. M. (Ed.). (1972). *Readings on the psychology of women.* New York: Harper & Row.

Benbow, C. P., & Stanley, J. C. (1980). Sex differences in mathematical ability: Fact or artifact? *Science, 210,* 1262–1264.

Birnbaum, J. A. (1975). Life patterns and self-esteem in gifted family-oriented and career-committed women. In M. T. S. Mednick, S. S. Tangri, & L. W. Hoffman (Eds.), *Women and achievement* (pp. 396–419). New York: John Wiley.

Brush, L. (September 2, 1982). Personal Communication.

Callahan, C. M. (1979). The gifted and talented woman. In A. H. Passow (Ed.), *The gifted and talented* (pp. 401–423). Chicago: National Society for the Study of Education.

Casserly, P. L. (1975). *An assessment of factors affecting female participation in advanced placement programs in mathematics, chemistry, and physics.* Report of National Science Foundation. (Grant GY-11325). Princeton, NJ: Educational Testing Service.

Clance, P. R. (1985). The imposter phenomenon. *New Woman, 15*(7), 40–43.

Coleman, J. (1961). *The adolescent society.* New York: Free Press.

Davis, J. A. (1964). Great aspirations: *The school plans of American's college seniors.* Chicago: Aldine.

Deaux, K., & Emswiller, T. (1974). Explanations of successful performance in sex-linked tasks: What's skill for the male is luck for the female. *Journal of Personality and Social Psychology, 29,* 80–85.

Dembart, L. (1984, March 7). Science: Social and cultural factors limit women's job opportunities. *Los Angeles Times*, p. 2.

Fennema, E. (1974). Mathematics learning and the sexes: *A review. Journal for Research in Mathematics Education, 5,* 126–139.

Fennema, E., & Sherman, J. (1977). Sex related differences in mathematics achievement spatial visualization and affective factors. *American Educational Research Journal, 14,* 51–71.

Fitzgerald, L. F., & Crites, J. O. (1980). Toward a career psychology of women: What do we know? What do we need to know? *Journal of Counseling Psychology, 27,* 44–62.

Fitzpatrick, J. L. (1978). Academic underachievement, other-direction, and attitudes toward women's roles in bright adolescent females. *Journal of Educational Psychology, 70(4),* 645–650.

Fox, L. H. (1977). Sex differences: Implications for program planning for the academically gifted. In J. C. Stanley, W. C. George, & C. H. Solano (Eds.), *The gifted and the creative: A fifty year perspective* (pp. 113–138). Baltimore, MD: Johns Hopkins University Press.

Gilligan, C. (1982). *In a different voice.* Cambridge, MA: Harvard University.

Goleman, D. (1980a, February). Still learning from Terman's children. *Psychology Today, 13(9),* 44–53.

Goleman, D. (1980b, February). 1,528 little geniuses and how they grew. *Psychology Today, 13(9),* 28–43.

Groth, N. J. (1975). Success and creativity in male and female professors. *Gifted Child Quarterly, 19,* 328–335.

Gysbers, M., Johnston, J., & Gust, T. (1968). Characteristics of homemaker and career-oriented women. *Journal of Counseling Psychology, 15(6),* 541–546.

Hauser, R. M. (1971). *Socioeconomic background and educational performance.* Washington, DC: American Sociological Association.

Hoffman, L. W. (1977). Fear of success in 1965 and 1974: A follow-up study. *Journal of Consulting and Clinical Psychology, 45,* 310–321.

Hollinger, C. L., & Fleming, E. S. (1984). Internal barriers to the realization of potential correlates and interrelationships among gifted and talented female adolescents. *Gifted Child Quarterly, 28,* 135–139.

Horner, M. S. (1972). Toward an understanding of achievement related conflicts in women. *Journal of Social Issues, 28,* 157–175.

Just how the sexes differ. (1981, May 18). *Newsweek,* p. 72–83.

Kramer, L. R. (1985). Social interaction and perceptions of ability: A study of gifted adolescent females. Paper presented at the annual meeting of the American Educational Research Association. Chicago, Illinois.

Lavach, J. F., & Lanier, H. B. (1975). The motive to avoid success in 7th, 8th, 9th, and 10th grade high-achieving girls. *The Journal of Educational Research, 68,* 216–218.

Leroux, J. A. (1985). *Gender differences influencing gifted adolescents: An ethnographic study of cultural expectations.* Unpublished doctoral dissertation, University of Connecticut, Storrs.

Maccoby, E. E., & Jacklin, C. N. (1974). *The psychology of sex differences.* Stanford, CA: Stanford University Press.

Machlowitz, M. (1982). The great imposters. *Working Women, 7(2),* 97–98.

O'Keefe, D. (July 25, 1985). Personal Communication.

Pallas, A. M., & Alexander, K. L. (1983). Sex differences in quantitative SAT performance: New evidence on the differential coursework hypothesis. *American Educational Research Journal, 20,* 165–182.

Parsons, J. E., Ruble, D. N., Hodges, K. L., & Small, A. (1976). Cognitive-developmental factors in emerging sex differences in achievement-related expectancies. *Journal of Social Issues, 32,* 47–61.

Pogrebin, L. C. (1980). Dear old sexist days: The fourth 'r is role-playing. *In Growing up free: Raising your child in the 80's* (pp. 491–518). New York: McGraw-Hill.

Rodenstein, J., Pfleger, L., & Colangelo, N. (1977). Career development needs of the gifted: Special consideration for gifted women. *Gifted Child Quarterly, 20,* 340–347.

Sadker, M. & D. (1985). Sexism in the schoolroom of the '80's. *Psychology Today, 19(3),* 54–57.

Schmidt, P. J. (1982). Sexist schooling. *Working Woman, 7*(10), 101–102.

Schwartz, L. L. (1980). Advocacy for the neglected gifted: Females. *Gifted Child Quarterly, 24,* 113–117.

Sears, P. S., & Barbee, A. H. (1977). Career and life satisfactions among Terman's gifted women. In J. S. Stanley, W. C. George, & C. H. Solano (Eds.), *The gifted and the creative: A fifty year perspective* (pp. 28–65). Baltimore, MD: Johns Hopkins University Press.

Shaw, M. C., & McCuen, J. T. (1960). The onset of academic underachievement in bright children. *Journal of Educational Psychology, 51,* 103–108.

Staines, G., Tavris, C., & Jayaratne, C. (1974). The queen bee syndrome. *Psychology Today, 7,* 55–60.

Stein, A. H., & Bailey, M. M. (1973). The socialization of achievement orientation in females. *Psychological Bulletin, 80,* 345–366.

Stockard, J. (1980). Why sex inequalities exist for students. In J. Stockard, P. A. Schmuck, K. Kempner, P. Williams, S. K. Edson, & M. A. Smith (Eds.), *Sex equity in education.* New York: Academic Press.

Stockard, J., & Wood, J. W. (1984). The myth of female underachievement: A reexamination of sex differences in academic underachievement. *American Educational Research Journal, 21,* 825–838.

Tobias, S. (1982). Sexist quotations. *Psychology Today, 16*(1), 14–17.

Warschaw, T. (1985). The "I-don't-deserve-it" syndrome. *New Women, 15* (4), 134–137.

White, W. L. (1984). *The perceived effects of an early enrichment experience: A forty year follow-up study of the Speyer School experiment for gifted students.* Unpublished doctoral dissertation, University of Connecticut, Storrs.

Wolleat, P. L. (1979). Guiding the career development of gifted females. In N. Colangelo & R. T. Zaffran (Eds.), *New voices in counseling the gifted.* Dubuque, IA: Kendall/Hunt.

6

Gifted and Gay: A Study of the Adolescent Experience

Jean Sunde Peterson

Purdue University

Heather Rischar

Truman State University

A retrospective study of the adolescent experience of 18 gay, lesbian, or bisexual young adults with high ability (12 males, 6 females) using a postpositivistic mode of inquiry found significant themes of danger, isolation, depression, and suicidal ideation, together with high achievement and extreme involvement in activities, in their narrative responses to an extended questionnaire. Participants described

Editor's Note: From Peterson, J. S., & Rischar, H. (2000). Gifted and gay: A study of the adolescent experience. *Gifted Child Quarterly*, 44(4), 231-246. © 2000 National Association for Gifted Children. Reprinted with permission.

personal responses to wondering about sexual orientation, being convinced, and eventually coming out, and the effects on school and family relationships. Half reported awareness by the end of elementary school, and almost all were convinced by grade 11. Most participants offered suggestions for educators in general and for those involved in gifted programs, and many of the suggestions have implications for staff development.

There has been only rare attention in gifted-education literature to the experience of being both gifted and gay/lesbian/bisexual (e.g., Friedrichs, 1997; Tolan, 1997). However, if estimates that 10% of the population may be homosexual and that one in five families has a gay or lesbian child (e.g., Dahlheimer & Feigal, 1991) are accurate, then it is likely that 10% of those identified as gifted are homosexual, as well, and that they and their extended families experience the emotional consequences of association with a stigmatized sexual orientation (Fontaine & Hammond, 1996). Aware of the gap in the literature, the researchers in this retrospective study sought to explore the experience of being both gifted and gay/lesbian/bisexual (hereafter referred to as GLB) in the interest of contributing to the knowledge base and discovering areas worthy of further study.

RELEVANT RESEARCH

Providing a foundation for exploring the intersection of giftedness and gayness is the literature that addresses, for example, giftedness as related to hypersensitivity (Lovecky, 1992), perfectionism (Hewitt, Newton, Flett, & Callander, 1997), emotional intensity (Piechowski, 1997), stress (Ferguson, 1981), depression (Webb, Meckstroth, & Tolan, 1982), and suicide (Farrell, 1989; Hayes & Sloat, 1989; Weisse, 1990). An additional connection between giftedness and gayness is the reality that, during high school, adaptation to uncertainty about sexual orientation may take socially acceptable forms such as academic or athletic overachievement, perfectionism, or overinvolvement in extracurricular activities (Harbeck, 1994), characteristics often associated with individuals perceived to be gifted. However, according to this study, high-ability adolescents are unlikely to discuss sexual orientation with significant adults in their lives.

Putting the Research to Use

The findings in this exploratory study argue that all gifted children and adolescents could benefit from discussion and information about sexuality, sexual orientation, and sexual-identity development, given the cited literature concerning both giftedness and gayness and given the complexity of physical, social, and emotional development. It is important that parents and educators understand that those individuals with particular concerns about their own development, including those who are convinced that they are gay/lesbian/bisexual (GLB), may feel isolated, may fear abandonment by peers and family, may be extreme achievers, may be severely depressed, and probably do not discuss their concerns with their parents or other significant adults.

All educators, particularly those involved in education for the gifted, need to be courageous in their support of GLB students, ensuring that their classrooms are physically and psychologically safe and intervening on behalf of students who are "out" or are bullied or teased because their behavior fit popular GLB stereotypes. Even quiet acknowledgement that gayness is worthy of discussion, that some respected individuals in textbooks are/were GLB, that concerns about sexual orientation are common during childhood and adolescence, and that GLB individuals are probably present in all schools and classrooms may help to lessen the distress of those who believe that no one has ever felt as they do. The findings in this study also urge parents, teachers, and school and community counselors to consider the possible link of sexual-orientation issues to substance abuse, dropping out, and suicidal ideation.

Sexuality and the Gifted

Sexual development is an important part of a child's making cognitive, emotional, and physical sense of the world. Yet parents may be uncomfortable discussing concerns about sexuality with their child (Roeper, 1997). Educators, including those in gifted education, may be similarly uncomfortable, as is perhaps reflected in the dearth of gifted-education literature related to sexuality in general, However, according to Tolan (1997), various affective areas related to giftedness, including androgyny, developmental asynchrony, early awareness of and concern about the complexity of sexuality, nonstereotypical gender behavior, and intensity of relationships, may contribute to confusion and fear about sexual identity, with effects on sexual behavior and development, including premature self-labeling. Though it has long been accepted that same-sex sexual behavior is not unusual during childhood (cf. Kinsey, Pomeroy, & Martin, 1948) and that sexuality is an area of flux for teens, lack of discussion or available information may, in fact, contribute to premature developmental foreclosure (Fontaine & Hammond, 1996). Tolan observed that the gifted may try to lessen their confusion through sexual experimentation or rejecting sexuality altogether.

Differentness and Isolation

There is another possible junction of giftedness and gayness. Exceptional ability may contribute to a sense of differentness, with a consequent impact on social relationships (Cross, Coleman & Stewart, 1995; Cross, Coleman, & Terharr-Yonkers, 1991; Webb, Meckstroth, & Tolan, 1982). When a gifted child is also GLB, that sense of differentness likely intensifies. In fact, social, emotional, and cognitive isolation was found to be the most frequent presenting problem at The Institute for the Protection of Lesbian and Gay Youth in New York City (Hetrick & Martin, 1987). The fact that GLB adolescents must generally find an identity and move to sexual and social maturation without role models and discussions available to heterosexual peers (Schneider, 1989) may exacerbate feelings of isolation and differentness already experienced by those with high ability. They also may have difficulty finding partners compatible with both sexual identity and intellectual capacity. If individuals are predisposed to isolation and lack of support, as many highly able adolescents are, sexuality issues may be life-threatening (Tolan, 1997).

The relationship between differentness and problems in self-esteem (Sullivan & Schneider, 1987) and between low self-esteem and suicide (McFarland, 1998) has also been discussed. Despite these concerns, until recently in the United States, "society has traditionally suppressed and ignored the social state of being homosexual, especially among adolescents, apart from the stigma and being pariah" (Herdt, 1989, p. 22). From 1977 to 1993, only three articles on GLB adolescents were published in *The School Counselor* (Fontaine & Hammond, 1996). However, an issue of *Professional School Counseling* (Baker & Campbell, 1998) devoted to sexual minority youth represents increasing attention to school and other concerns of GLB adolescents. There has also been interest in comparing GLB concerns cross-culturally (e.g., Herdt, 1989; Ross, 1989; Rotheram-Borus, Hunter, & Rosario, 1994). Related to this interest is an awareness that some segments of minority communities believe that all gay people are White, thereby compounding the lack of access to accurate information about homosexuality by adolescents of color (Fontaine & Hammond, 1996).

Almost all pertinent literature comes from journals not specifically related to education for the gifted. An examination of that literature provides a backdrop for the areas of focus in the current study: school issues, self-destructive behavior, sexual-identity formation and other developmental issues, the process of coming out, and strategies for support.

School Issues

The School Climate. School for GLB adolescents may be uncomfortable at best and dangerous at worst. Adolescents must simultaneously deal with two developmental tasks, growing up and developing sexual identity, while at the same time hearing homophobic stereotypes and taunts and witnessing humiliation and violence (Zera, 1992). They hear derogatory labels for homosexuals being applied to anyone who is disliked, and adolescent emotional liability and lack of accurate information about homosexuality exacerbate fears (Fontaine & Hammond, 1996). Butler (1994) found that teachers not only lacked knowledge about homosexuality, but also generally held slightly homophobic attitudes and were unwilling to address GLB issues or behave in supportive ways.

Danger. In addition, GLB adolescents are likely to experience verbal and physical harassment, including bullying (Baldauf, 1997). One in six gay students is beaten badly enough to seek medical attention, 20% skip school at least once a month because of fear, and, in one city, 28% dropped out of school (Bart, 1998). In fact, homophobia may be more vicious in high schools than in any other institution. One-third of GLB high school students surveyed had experienced direct violence due to their sexual identities (Elia, 1993). Straight students, too, may suffer from anti-gay abuse, a result of not fitting gender stereotypes, such as female athletes and males interested in dance or theater (Bart, 1998). Savin-Williams (1994) found that incidents of harassment were sometimes instigated by faculty, staff, and administrators in schools, and Griffin (1994) reported intense homophobia in athletics. Hodges, Malone, and Perry (1997) found that victimization occurred when children had few friends, had friends who were incapable of fulfilling a protective function, or were rejected by peers. Hetrick and Martin (1987), studying 329 GLB adolescents, found that one-third had experienced violence. However, 49% of that violence was at the hands of the family.

Depression and Self-Destructive Behaviors

Probably as a result of the milieu just described, sexual orientation has been increasingly connected to suicide (e.g., Fontaine, 1998; Gibson, 1989; Hammelman, 1993; Hershberger, Pilkington, & D'Augelli, 1997; Lock, 1998; Poppenhagen & Qualley, 1998). Difficulties related to increased self-awareness of sexual orientation are reflected in one finding that 39% of GLB adolescents had attempted suicide, and 52% of these had made more than one attempt (Rotheramo-Borus et al., 1994). According to various sources (Fontaine, 1998; Kissen, 1993; McFarland, 1998), one in three adolescent suicides may be attributed to sexual identity issues. It should be noted, however, that suicide completions and attempts by adolescents decrease with age (Hetrick & Martin, 1987).

Suicide among GLB adolescents may be attributed to feelings of disenfranchisement, social isolation, rejection by family and peers, and self-revulsion

(Savin-Williams, 1994). The oppression and stigma associated with homosexuality in a homophobic environment can contribute to and exacerbate problems of low self-esteem, isolation, guilt, depression, difficulty with creating identity (Fontaine, 1998), and perfectionism (Harbeck, 1994). Internalized homophobia, an intense self-contempt resulting from extreme homophobia in the schools (Elia, 1993) may be a factor in all of these (Lock, 1998).

In general, indirect self-destructive behavior, including substance abuse, running away from home, smoking, and risky sexual behavior, appears to be associated with the stress of having a stigmatized sexual orientation (Ferguson, 1981; McCarthy, Brack, Laygo, Brack, & Orr, 1997). It is also difficult for teens to join the larger gay subculture, since most activities are adult-oriented (Zera, 1992). According to Schneider (1989), the "alcohol-focused, sexually loaded environment" (p. 126) of the bar scene, which "bypasses the gradual and safe ways in which most heterosexual youngsters learn to deal with alcohol and sexual intimacy" (p. 127) is "not appropriate for young people, and they themselves know it" (p. 126).

Sexual-Identity Formation

The researchers recognize that assuming a consensus concerning the meaning of the phrase sexual identity is unwise, given the related, ongoing essentialism-constructionism debate among psychologists (e.g., Bohan, 1996). Nevertheless, theorists who have explored the sexual-identity construct will be discussed here. Schneider (1989) proposed five stages of sexual-identity development: growing awareness of homosexual feelings and identity; developing positive evaluations of homosexuality; developing intimate same-sex romantic/erotic relationships; establishing social ties with GLB peers or community; and self-disclosure. Cass (1979) theorized that GLB youth progress through six stages: confusion (involving questioning and searching for information), comparison, tolerance, acceptance, pride, and synthesis. Adolescence is not necessarily the time for *expression* of sexual identity, but the awareness exists (Waldnor-Haugrud, & Magruder, 1996). In fact, children as young as 5 or 6 may know they are somehow different in sexual orientation (Cantwell, 1997). According to Zera (1992), GLB adolescents may cope by identifying themselves as heterosexual or becoming gender deviant, exaggerating stereotypical homosexual characteristics out of a belief that this is how gay people dress or behave. They may also test their orientation with intercourse with the other gender, basing their conclusions on whether the experience is emotionally satisfying (Edwards, 1996).

Evans and Levine (1990) proposed that timing, duration, and outcome of sexual identity formation are affected by internal and external factors: the social context, degree of peer and family support, and psychological adjustment of the individual involved. Edwards (1996) found support for the fact that GLB adolescents can operate with good social adjustment in heterosexual society, identifying and disclosing to whatever degree seems necessary, if they accept and develop an explanation of who they are and can withstand the homophobic attitudes they will experience. However, Fontaine (1998) noted that the time of identity confusion represents high potential for suicide attempts. Uribe (1994) focused on the vulnerability of middle school GLB students in the school environment, in line with findings that awareness of sexual orientation occurs at or before puberty (Anderson, 1987; Benvenuti, 1986). In fact, age 10 has been noted as a time of significant hormonal development, with implications for the development of sexual attraction, cognition, emotions, motivations, and social behavior (McClintock & Herdt, 1996).

The idea of disenfranchised grief applies here, a type of grief that is not acceptable or understood by others in the culture. As GLB individuals struggle with sexual identity, during adolescence, they often anticipate loss of friends, family support, identity, a vision of their own self-worth (Lenhardt, 1997), and their church (Ritter & O'Neal, 1989). Gifted GLB adolescents, who may feel a responsibility to be perfect (cf. Hewitt et al., 1997), may also have a sense of failure as they contemplate an identity unacceptable to others (Coleman & Remafedi, 1989; Fontaine & Hammond, 1996; Schneider, 1989; Sullivan & Schneider, 1987). Lack of role models may exacerbate their stress. In regard to the intersection of gayness and giftedness, Kissen (1993) observed that GLB teens carry a double burden of being part of an oppressed minority and knowing absolutely no one like themselves. Based on Kissen's comments, gifted GLB students might then carry a triple burden.

Lock (1998) offered a developmental framework, reflecting these burdens, through a case study of a gifted gay male adolescent with internalized homophobia. At age 12–14, the client experienced depression, preoccupation with gay stereotypes, and unconscious seeking of externalized homophobia to relieve internal discomfort. He also avoided leaving the family because of anxiety about peer acceptance, with that anxiety contributing to volatile emotional responses to the family. At age 14–16, there was increased depression, as well as heightened needs for and frustration about peer relationships. Later came a sense of hopelessness about the future, self-destructive behavior, a sense that high school would never end, and ambivalence about leaving home and about future opportunities for intimacy. Eventually, he was able to integrate personal aspects of the self with gay-group identity.

Coming Out

The current study was interested in family and school experiences surrounding the "coming out" process. Among the earliest to address this phenomenon, deMonteflores and Schultz (1978) defined it as "the developmental process through which gay people recognize their sexual preferences and choose to integrate this knowledge into their personal and social lives" (p. 60). Ben-Ari (1995) found that most GLB individuals came out to one parent first, most often the mother. Fears about coming out stemmed from the irreversible nature of disclosure, and fear of rejection was the most frequently mentioned fear. The mean age of coming out was 21. The most common reason for coming out was "not to hide, not to live a lie" (p. 310). However, according to Poppenhagen and Qualley (1998), coming out may move a person from a socially approved and validated existence to a socially condemned and oppressed existence, a loss of status. Such loss, including loss of face, may lead to suicide. Herdt (1989) noted that the closeness of coming out to puberty or to separating from parents' households contributes to experiencing these situations as crises.

Parents often experience grief after a son or daughter has come out to them because they have lost some of their hopes for the future for their child, the essence of whom has changed for them (Borhek, 1993). Cramer and Roach (1988) found that most parents initially reacted negatively to the disclosure, but became more accepting over time. The majority of participants in their study reported having a more positive relationship with mothers than with fathers, both before and after coming out. In general, a positive prior relationship with parents predicts a healthy resolution (Borhek), and parents who perceive that disclosure is within the context of intimacy adjust more easily than when otherwise disclosed (Ben-Ari, 1995).

Given the aforementioned lack of literature addressing the co-incidence of gayness and giftedness and recognizing that parents may indeed idealize a gifted child (Cornell, 1984), drawing parallels between coming out as gifted and coming out as GLB should be done only cautiously and should certainly acknowledge that such parallels might trivialize the great difficulties associated with coming out as GLB. Being labeled "gifted" may indeed be stigmatizing and may have mixed effects on parent, sibling, and peer relationships (Colangelo & Brower, 1987). In fact, parents may "closet" their child's abilities because of community attitudes (Webb et al., 1982). Gifted individuals themselves may hide abilities, managing information about themselves in response to the threat of the potentially stigmatizing association with giftedness (Cross, Coleman, & Stewart, 1995). In this regard, Mahoney's (1998) Gifted Identity Formation Model, which can serve as a guide for understanding gifted individuals, emphasizes that it is important to be aware of how giftedness is valued in the individual's environment. Among the constructs that this model emphasizes are validation (acknowledgement of giftedness by self or others), affirmation (interactive acknowledgment and reinforcement), and affiliation (alliance with others who are similar). These constructs may be applied to GLB identity development, as well. Important relationships are the source for validation, affirmation, and affiliation. Problems in these relationships, including significant others' issues regarding sexual orientation, undoubtedly have an impact on sexual-identity formation. Given the difficulties associated with unsupportive contexts in each case, it may be assumed that self-validating and coming out as *both* gifted and gay may present especially formidable challenges.

Other Aspects of Development

Unfortunately, there is a lack of understanding of what is normative in regard to GLB development, with a notable lack of research looking at changes that occur as GLB youth move into adulthood (Edwards, 1996), including in adolescents and young adults who were physically or emotionally abused by peers or family (Boxer & Cohler, 1989). The majority of research on gay and lesbian development has involved retrospective studies with adult males (Zera, 1992) and has been based on individuals in counseling and support groups (Edwards, 1996). In quantitative studies, sample sizes have often been small, and heterosexual comparison groups have not always been utilized (Zera, 1992). Qualitative methodology has been used relatively recently to build theory of GLB development (e.g., Ben-Ari, 1995; Kissen, 1993; Omizo, Omizo, & Okamoto, 1998; Schneider, 1989) and to learn how gifted children and adolescents cope with pressures (Sowa & May, 1997).

Uribe and Harbeck (1992) found that all of the 50 self-identified GLB high school students in their study felt that their social development had been seriously inhibited by their homosexuality. These authors asserted that GLB adolescents may be

> at a higher risk of dysfunction because of unfulfilled developmental needs for identification with a peer group, lack of positive role modeling influences and experiences, negative societal pressures, and their dependence upon parents and educators who may be unwilling or unable to provide emotional support concerning the issue of homosexuality. (p. 16)

Strategies for Support

As a result of increased attention to GLB adolescents, strategies have been proposed for support of this at-risk population. These strategies have included educating service providers (Schneider & Tremble, 1986) and school staff (Schwartz, 1994) and encouraging self-examination in regard to homophobia and biases concerning differences (Dunham, 1989); implementing policies protecting GLB students from discrimination and violence (Bart, 1998); establishing distance support networks (Bridget & Lucille, 1996) and out-of-school (Singerline, 1994) and school support groups; providing information about health and other concerns (Cranston, 1992); altering curricula to include references to GLB historical and literary figures (Schwartz, 1994; Sumara, 1993); making literature related to GLB adolescent concerns available (Hanckel & Cunningham, 1976); and providing therapeutic interventions (e.g., Bradish, 1995; Kottman, Lingg, & Tisdell, 1995). Appropriate counseling can address concerns about sexual identity and explore daydreams, sexual experiences, affectional patterns, unexpressed attractions, and emotional responses (Fontaine & Hammond, 1996).

Purpose

The purpose of this exploratory and mostly qualitative study was to examine the adolescent experience of high-ability GLB individuals, both male and female, through a retrospective look at school and family experiences from grades 5–12, in order to better understand the development of gifted GLB adolescents, to gain knowledge that might be helpful to educators and counselors of gifted GLB adolescents with high ability, and to illuminate areas that might warrant further study. It was not within the scope of this study to compare these individuals' experiences with those of non-GLB young adults, but rather to focus on the phenomenological experience of a particular group of individuals. In keeping with the grounded-theory methodology used in this study (Glasser & Strauss, 1967), the study sought to provide a perspective on behavior; to enable description, prediction, and explanation of behavior; to present findings usable in practical applications and understandable to practitioners; and to develop tentative hypotheses concerning the adolescent experience of being both gibed and GLB.

Participants

Participants were 18 young adults (6 females and 12 males), age 18–25, ethnicity unknown, who self-identified as both gifted and gay/lesbian/bisexual. Gifted GLB individuals willing to be open about sexual orientation were difficult to access. The researchers decided that self-identification would be necessary. In addition, for a variety of reasons, participants would not be given criteria for giftedness, such as grade-point average, test scores, or identification for a special program. They would likely come from a wide variety of high schools, with similar GPAs potentially varying in meaning. It could not be assumed that participants would know their scores on intelligence tests; their schools might, in fact, not have conducted individual assessment; and their schools might not have identified gifted children for special programs. It appeared that not only was no common measure available for determining giftedness, but there would also be no way of ascertaining that participants met particular criteria. Recognizing the wide variety of ways the construct *giftedness* can be defined (Peterson, 1999), the study would nevertheless rely on participants' assessment of self in relation to peers in a university setting, if they had not been identified as gifted during the school years.

Instrument

Participants filled out a nonstandardized 10-page questionnaire containing 13 questions, each with several parts, for a total of 70 separate items (see Appendix). The questionnaire required 1–4 hours to complete. Approximately half of the questions were open-ended and were intended to generate narrative data. With rare exceptions, participants answered these questions at length. The other questions elicited yes/no or other brief responses. The questionnaire was developed with particular interest in respondents' perceptions of their own social, emotional, and sexual-identity development; of others' responses to them as they developed; and of giftedness as related to sexual identity. Current literature also informed the development of the questionnaire.

METHOD

Two researchers conducted the study. Participants responded to a mailing to GLB support groups at eight midwestern college or university campuses and to a presentation to one such large group at a highly selective institution. All of these contacts extended an invitation to gifted GLB individuals to participate in the study. Questionnaires were returned by mail.

Data were analyzed either quantitatively (yes/no responses and responses relating to age, grade level, or time interval), using percentages, or qualitatively (narrative responses), the latter process utilizing Glasser and Strauss's (1967) constant comparative method of qualitative analysis. The narrative responses were initially read by each researcher individually, with each questionnaire read as a unit, and with attention to general impressions. Responses were then organized so that all answers to each question were grouped together. These grouped responses were then analyzed qualitatively by each researcher independently for themes, each using an inductive process by which "categories emerge" and "data emerge that fit an existing category" (Glasser & Strauss, 1967), and each using an independently created color-coding scheme. Subsequently, the researchers compared coding schemes and the themes that had emerged for each question and for the questionnaire in general. The various similarly coded language segments were then clustered according to developing themes and were continually reclustered and studied.

In all, the data underwent some degree of analysis six times, the last four analyses in the interest of regrouping into ever broader clusters and integrating themes in responses to individual questions with general questionnaire themes (e.g., the theme of danger, which was the specific focus of one question, but which also appeared in various forms at several other points in the questionnaire). The researchers experienced considerable agreement at each stage of the process, including identification of both major themes and clusters, although each researcher had independently also located particular minor strands, which became part of later clusters. "Disagreement" generally occurred only in terms of word choice for labeling themes and clusters and was not quantified.

RESULTS

Differentness and Isolation

Themes of differentness and isolation emerged, with a variety of contributing factors articulated: social awkwardness, level of maturity, ability and interests, depression, and behavioral choice. Some specifically mentioned sexual orientation as contributing to social withdrawal, and a few indicated feelings of guilt and shame. One male "avoided parties, drinking, sex, etc., both for solid moral reasons and out of fear—at least discomfort." A female wrote, "I felt constantly alone—separated myself from my peers as a way of coping with the prejudice, name-calling, etc." One male's response noted a change during junior high: "In fifth grade I was generally pretty happy. I was stable. By eighth grade I was beginning to feel depressed and isolated." Another male commented about eighth grade:

> I didn't fit in at all. Felt a lot of pain. I was constantly made fun of for being a "sissy," not being athletic, and not "fitting in" with the guys. I was suicidal in eighth grade because I felt like a sinner for finding other boys attractive. Guilt and shame were quite severe.

Junior high meant change for yet another:

> I was popular in fifth and sixth because I was smart. Really unpopular in seventh and eighth. I was in activities and had a few friends, but it was two of the worst years of my life socially. I actually was called Rocky—after Rock Hudson. That's when the rumors started.

One male reported,

> I was called "Pussy" because of my lack of interest in sports. I was more interested in music and academics, which was looked down upon by many people. At times, I emotionally and socially felt kind of "out of it."

One said he was "an outcast." Another male's response is typical of those connecting feelings of alienation, isolation, pain, and differentness to sexuality: "It's very difficult to adequately articulate thoughts of sexuality at a young age. It also separates you from many other people your own age." Only one participant specifically connected differentness to being both gay and gifted: "I think to be labeled 'gifted' means to be labeled as 'different,' which is what being gay essentially is. To be both is an interesting interaction indeed."

School Issues

Positive and Negative Experiences Associated with Sexual Orientation. One question asked about positive and negative experiences associated with sexual orientation. One female's statement captures the general thrust of the positive comments: "[Teachers] validated sexual orientation as an important topic to explore and understand." Females also cited school newspapers and classrooms that invited discussion of GLB issues, such as gays in the military, and one had had openly lesbian teachers. A female added an important note at the end of the questionnaire: "Surprisingly I've discovered not everyone's experiences were negative or painful." Males' positive comments all referred to experiences outside of school and included GLB support groups and a Sunday School unit about homosexuality.

Negative experiences did not always involve overt hostility. Some participants mentioned an uncomfortable classroom atmosphere or a perceived lack of support:

"My sexual orientation became an issue in debate class. I had to drop the class, and it kept me from joining other organizations in school."

"I was labeled a theater fag and never got male leads."

"Teachers squelched my desire to work with gay issues."

One participant cited the lack of reformation in school about safe sex, in light of the danger of HIV infection: "Health and wellness completely omitted all discussion of GLB health issues."

Danger. It should be noted here that five participants (28%) said they had felt no danger. However, supporting the considerable literature referring to hostility toward GLB students in school, most of the participants, 11 (61%) indicated that they had indeed felt danger—at school for 7 (39%). In regard to peers, a male commented, "Everywhere, in the halls between classes, in class, at lunch, before and after school, and at special school activities; the potential for danger was always there." Another said, "On a trip one person claimed he'd never speak to, or would beat up, a best friend or cousin if he 'turned queer on him.' Made me wonder how a really 'out' person would fare at school."

Also reflecting the literature, some experienced the hostility of teachers. A junior high physical education teacher made a degrading comment about a male to his classmates: "I was horrified. At that moment I realized that my peers weren't the only people I had to fear, but males of all ages. I left school and cried the entire day." Another wrote, "Teachers assaulted me for being gay, and no one cared." A teacher began a rumor about one male participant and later apologized.

Depression and Self-Destructive Behavior

The danger also came from within. Fifteen (83%) reported bouts with depression during junior and senior high school, and 13 (72%) reported being suicidal at some point during that time, although 5 (28%) noted improvement in emotional stability after grade 10. One female had experienced depression from 4th–12th grade, and another "pondered suicide in middle school, but never formulated a plan." High school was the time of vulnerability for nine (50%), with six (33%) reporting depression in grade 9, five (28%) in grade 10, and seven (39%) in grade 11. A male wrote, "I was afraid that I'd never have a meaningful relationship with anyone and that I would grow old and die alone and unhappy." Regarding telling someone, 12 (80%) of the 15 who experienced depression discussed depression with someone, mostly with a friend, a counselor, or both. Only 5 (33%) of the 15 told parents, and none told teachers. As for suicide, 11 (85%) of the 13 who reported suicidal ideation discussed it with friends, a counselor, or both, none with teachers, and only 4 (31%) with parents. For 11 of the 18 participants (61%), talking was one of many proactive strategies for coping with low morale. A male said, "I immersed myself in activities or work. Often these became artistically productive times." A female said, "I've learned to cry, and I do this well and quite often."

Of the 14 (78% of participants) who experienced counseling, 11 (79%) perceived it as helpful. Counseling occurred mostly during the high school years, and it was mostly sustained or intermittent over a period of 1–4 years. Some of those for whom counseling was helpful reported the following:

"It gave me someone to open up to and sort out my feelings."

"I was able to solidify good relationships with people and learn coping strategies."

"First session—knowing that my sexuality didn't make me sick.'"

"I began to love myself again and gain confidence."

One wished the counselor "could have clued me in to just how many people there were out there just like me—or shared some issues [that] clients who had come out to him had dealt with." Another wished the counselor had not "kept bringing up sexual orientation."

Sexual-Identity Formation

The age of first wondering about sexual orientation in this study supports the literature attesting to early awareness (e.g., Cantwell, 1997). Nine, exactly half, of the participants reported wondering about sexual orientation before leaving elementary school, with five (56%) of those nine noting sixth grade. Of the eight (44%) reporting junior or senior high awareness, four (50%) cited grades 8 and 9. All but one (94% of participants) reported *awareness* by grade 10, and that one person was aware in grade 12. In general, awareness was in the form of attraction, crushes, dreams, personal-journal themes, and realizing these weren't "just a passing phase." Nine (50%) reported that they responded to their awareness with some behavior, such as becoming "ultra-hetero" ("It made me nervous and scared, and I threw myself into my relationship with my boyfriend."), depressed ("I started having suicidal thoughts for the first time"; "I was taught it was a sin and you would go to hell. I was quite depressed and wanted to end my life"), seriously anti-gay, or pouring energies into achievement. Two males (17% of male participants) quit sports out of fear of others or of their own feelings, and two more males reported that they feared peers during sports activities. Nine (50% of participants) were "OK" with the awareness. One male reported, "I filed it away in my consciousness. It was all wrapped up in the general curiosity/excitement/ embarrassment of sexual discovery and puberty."

A minor theme of absence, rather than presence, of expected feelings emerged. Five males (42% of male participants) believed they had the "same feelings" as their peers, but had an absence of feelings for females ("I had tons of gay fantasies. I had no desire to date girls although I pretended to"; "I liked being with girls, but I had no desire to be with them physically. I found boys quite exciting and found them physically beautiful"). Several noted that their awareness was not a great concern prior to puberty: "I learned it was 'normal' for boys to wonder, and many experimented together around this age, so I thought it was OK as long as I liked girls, too. Wasn't too big of an issue for a couple years."

Regarding sexual identity, there was much self-analysis, perceived pressure, fear, and either-or thinking reported. The following experiences of males reflect various combinations of these:

> I got tendentious because I was trying to prove everything (my sexuality, my self-worth) by how well I played the cello, and consequently, was very tense. When I stopped concentrating on cello, it freed up a lot of time to concentrate on my sexuality. This led to a bravura attempt to think myself into one orientation or the other. Being a really all-or-nothing person back then, I thought I had to be perfectly gay or perfectly straight. This, of course, led to a dependence on living up to stereotypes in order to define who I was.

> I can't believe how long I actually believed that gays are supposed to be effeminate, speak with a lisp, not like sports, be always thinking about sex! What a massive form of thought control! I have been fortunate [in college] to meet some nonstereotypical gays who have been good role models for me.

> I didn't know being bisexual existed, so I was tumultuous over being just straight or gay. Incredibly indecisive, tons of anxiety as I got older, especially toward my father. I wanted to impress him, but we didn't like the same things or value the same things.

> I had no role models. Had to create them in my mind. Had to learn what gay was and then unlearn it, as society's stereotypes didn't fit with my personal expectations or desires.

A female worried, "I felt I couldn't have a real identity unless I labeled myself."

Other Aspects of Development

Growth and Maturity. In general, and in retrospect, development was difficult. The following comment reflects the impact of sexual-identity issues on growth and maturity: "Other kids got to have boyfriends and girlfriends and relationships that helped them mature and grow socially. Most gay youth are deprived of this." A particularly powerful comment summarizes the sexual-social interaction: "The difficulty is seriously compounded by the suspicion that the person you may be becoming will not be readily accepted by family, friends, and education."

Achievement. Academically, 14 (78%) were high achievers throughout school, and a major theme involved academic success as "balance" or "outlet." A male reported, "[I was] stable, but confused. [I] repressed a lot and focused on academics and activities to substitute for vulnerability, feelings, and experiences." Four other males said they were extreme achievers:

"Top of my class, hyper-involved in extra-curriculars. Since then, I've suspected much of that was avoiding dealing with orientation and socialization issues. In structured activities, I was safe."

"My retarded romantic and sexual development left a gap, which activities filled. High drive to succeed in measurable ways."

"I desperately needed something to excel at, and academics took its logical place as that thing. It was something I could always hold over everyone's head. I excelled."

"I always gave 150% to any school project. I was the definition of overachiever! It was important for me to impress my teachers and show up my classmates. Since I wasn't good at sports, I had to compensate!"

In contrast, one male considered dropping out of high school three times, and a female dropped out of school and then returned, ultimately graduating as an honor student. All four (22%) who were underachievers in high school became achievers in college.

Social Development. In general, high school was better socially than junior high, with improved relations for 12 (67%) of the 18. A female wrote, "Got more confident. Not sure exactly why. Volunteered at a hospital and got a job." Being a self-described extrovert and being involved in extracurricular activities helped several, and one female and one male found nonlocal friends through nonschool activities. Attending a summer scholars academy helped one male. However, as mentioned earlier, nine (50%) experienced depression during high school, one male experienced social rejection in 11th grade when he came out, and a few reported drug use. One female didn't want to date until she had figured out her sexual orientation, and another reported, "[I was] a wreck, always depressed, at times suicidal. It always seemed to be on my mind. I made two serious attempts. My emotional state was made worse by my attempts to hide it."

Awareness of same-gender attraction by grade 11 for 17 (94%) did not necessarily mean "being convinced" that they were GLB. However, 12 (67%) reported being convinced by grade 11, with grades 10 or 11 marking that turning point for 8 (44%) of the participants. Subsequently, of the 12 who were convinced in high school (but not necessarily "out"), 10 (83%) experienced negative effects on school life, and 6 (50%) felt that home communication was negatively affected—generally females with their mothers and males with their fathers. Three males reported the following:

"I became a big pile of anxiety, especially with my father, I never wanted to be home."

"I felt as if he wanted a 'son,' and I hadn't fulfilled his wishes."

"As I realized it wasn't a phase, that I was different, I could hardly be alone with him. We worked together on the farm, and it weighed heavy on me."

With peers, 4 (33%) of the 12 who became convinced in high school felt they went "downhill socially," while 7 (58%) reported being "OK" socially, with several continuing to pass as straight. With best friends, half reported no change, while two (17%) experienced a negative effect on the relationship, One female's best friend "said it was cool, but then stopped talking. I bought her a book about it, and then I became her token gay friend. She'd show me off. We no longer talk." A male explained, "I suppose I had mild crushes on a couple friends which were under the sexual threshold—expressed as intense loyalty, interest, joy." Another said, "I did what I could to prove I wasn't gay to them—locker room talk, experimenting with women. They never suspected anything." Another "had many girlfriends."

For seven (39%), "no one knew." One male remarked that not being effeminate helped him pass as heterosexual. Another reflected success with a common adolescent concern: "I wanted everyone to like me." A female said she "ended up dating a lot of men and insisting on my heterosexuality. I didn't come out or talk about it." In general, school became uncomfortable for several. One male became an expert at jokes and nervous laughter in his "homophobic all-male school," as he described it, repressed his feelings, and feared looking at anyone in the locker room. Another male quit sports and "didn't associate with guys too much other than really surface things. I was scared I might like them." Being convinced precipitated other varied responses as well:

"Grades suffered. I didn't know if I would be able to stay in school, knowing that I was gay."

"Always felt a need to try and become straight. I was oversensitive to comments by classmates. I felt oppressed at school and was absent frequently."

"If anyone had found out, I would have immediately killed myself. I drew away from people, became shy so they wouldn't notice my effeminacy."

One male "liked to befriend people who weren't as popular."

Special Needs as Gifted Adolescents. Addressing an area not unrelated to development, the questionnaire also asked whether high ability had created unique needs in them as GLB persons and whether they believed that hypersensitivity had been a factor during their adolescence. There was considerable reference to hyperawareness of labels, homophobia, reactions of others, and fear of the future. Regarding unique needs, one participant reported, "It narrowed the field of people I can relate to." Some reported a need to pursue information, and one worried about the effect of sexual orientation on career. One male said, "Sometimes I have felt overly competitive in terms of achievement, perhaps as a compensation for feeling inadequate or not accepted by society." Another commented, "My successes made me high profile and even more reluctant to explore a possibly scandalous sexuality."

The questionnaire also asked how participants had used their intelligence to enhance their lives and/or relate to society as a GLB person. Most felt they had used their intelligence proactively—writing, being politically active, being creative, being able to use humor and irony, reading and being informed, being able to "shift perspectives," and being able "to spar, debate, and argue with the most adroit gay basher."

Coming Out

Only one individual came out during junior high, and only four (22%) came out during high school. The incidence of depression during high school and the coming out at age 18 or beyond for 13 (72%) suggest that the coming-out process was preceded by stress and depression and that coming out occurred for most at the time of leaving home. Subsequently, there was less reported depression. Regarding coming out, parents of six (33%) were supportive, either initially or after some adjustment. Some parents "cried" or were "shocked" or "frightened." Some reacted with silence, the silence often continuing to the present. About the process for the family, one wrote, "It takes time." Siblings varied greatly in responses.

Peers were supportive for 11 (61%). A male commented, "I have been blessed with an extraordinarily strong network of peer support. Totally non-judgmental and accepting." Several mentioned finding comfort in close friendships with the other gender during this period, including one female who said, "My best friends turned out to be gay guys." However, one male wrote, "I had to move away from everyone I knew to begin coming out." A 25-year-old male reported, "I have yet to come out to my high school friends."

Eleven (61%) reported having good relationships since high school. GLB support groups in college became a place for unconditional acceptance and enhanced self-esteem for almost all. A male wrote. "If it hadn't been for college I would not be alive. I was at a critical point. College was my last hope."

Strategies for Support

In response to a question about what educators should understand about the school experiences of GLB adolescents, three comments are typical:

"Know there's so much going on in their heads."

"They need role models."

"There is almost no support for coming out of the closet."

Most respondents instead gave specific suggestions to educators.

1. "Let them know they're OK." "Let them know they are not 'bad,' 'evil,' 'sick.'"

2. "Let them know they're not alone. To have known even one gay person would have helped, or to have had famous or respected people come

out of the closet, or to have had the gay-friendly movies of the last few years"; "I wish I had had a couple of other gays I could ask the questions I had"; "When students read Tennessee Williams, mention his sexuality, if for no other reason than to know it's out there."

3. "Entertain the reality of gayness more. I wish all educators could look out at a classroom with an understanding that there probably are GLB students—who are proud, scared, confused, in love with someone of the same gender, lonely."

4. "Be alert to the possibility that sexual orientation may be the reason for someone's being suicidal, being involved with substance abuse, or dropping out."

5. "Treat them with compassion. They have rough lives. It's amazing any of them survive."

6. "Never show disappointment or dismissal of youths' sexual feelings."

7. "Challenge their overinvolvement. I suppose I was such a model student that they didn't feel an urge to change anything."

8. "Ask, 'Is my classroom safe, respectful?'"

9. "Stop the name-calling in the classroom. Say something!"

GLB Issues and Gifted Education

The questionnaire asked whether gifted education should give attention to GLB issues. All participants supported that focus. The following comments are typical and thought-provoking:

"Gifted education, in my experience, has been open to controversial issues. Therefore, it seems there would be room to explore these issues."

"I think gifted education would be a good place to explore sexuality concerns because of the greater ability of students to think through the subject."

"Gifted GLB students who aren't secure in themselves are at great risk for suicide and other emotional problems. Not everybody had the liberal, confidence-raising family that I did."

"Many people who realize their homosexuality at a young age are gifted."

"There are a lot of us."

DISCUSSION

Even for mainstream adolescents, normal developmental tasks can be complex and difficult. For GLB adolescents, meeting developmental challenges is particularly lonely and daunting, according to this study. For almost all in this study, problems with identity development affected sense of self and were associated with depression, which in turn affected social relationships. Social discomfort was associated with isolation for many, and "wondering," even before leaving elementary school, precipitated social uneasiness for many.

The process that eventually led to coming out was fraught with anxiety for most. However, facing the perceived, and probably real, possibility of rejection by family as a result of revelations about sexual orientation may have contributed to earlier-than-expected differentiation from family: GLB young people had soberly faced the prospect of a life apart from them. In general, these participants survived alone, with no role models, no GLB peers, and no one or very few with whom they could share their feelings and thoughts, especially during the years of "wondering," but also after being convinced of sexual orientation. With so much that was hidden and so much silence, there was risk: depression and suicidal ideation, dropping out of school, and substance abuse. On the other hand, many of these participants appeared to have developed resilience through their intense struggles during adolescence and, as young adults, expressed optimism about the future. It should be noted that none reported negative effects of self-described "overinvolvement" in activities as they compensated for discomfort and perceived deficiency, although one advised educators to challenge such involvement.

It is difficult to ascertain to what degree the intersection of gayness and giftedness complicated these participants' lives. Few alluded to their high ability when responding to questions concerning social and emotional development. However, specific questions about ability in terms of coping, hypersensitivity, special needs, and attention to sexual orientation in gifted education elicited a great amount of narrative. Nevertheless, parallels should be drawn between gayness and giftedness only cautiously in terms of sense of differentness, various developmental issues, and threats to well-being. Both factors may be stigmatized, in some contexts more than others, and both have the potential for contributing to difficulties. Being both gifted and gay means being doubly different, if not more so, with each quality potentially exacerbating the difficulties associated with the other. Yet, according to both the existing literature and to the data here concerning the safety of GLB individuals and the effects of a GLB sexual identity on social and emotional development, it is unwise to consider giftedness and gayness as equally problematic, no matter how atypical those in either category are in the general population. In spite of that caution, however, it is important to consider how gayness affects the social and emotional development of gifted individuals amid the demands of adolescent development. Whether a gay-gifted intersection doubly warns against expressing abilities, or whether consequent anxiety contributes to extreme school involvement and achievement, it should be recognized that the authentic self may be hidden—at great personal cost.

None of these participants talked to a teacher about depression or thoughts of suicide as adolescents, and few talked to parents. These findings raise questions for both educators in general and educators of the gifted. Do gifted GLB children and adolescents have too much invested in an image of competence and achievement to reveal vulnerabilities? Are teachers seen as interested only in curriculum, academics, and productivity? In addition, how can educators, school counselors, and parents explore sexuality and sexual orientation with youth at enough length that young people will be able to approach these subjects with a significant adult when they have questions and concerns? The findings here argue for staff development in listening and responding skills. Several suggestions offered by the participants in this study could serve as directions for in-servicing educators, crucial in meeting the needs expressed in this study. Current research should also be incorporated, especially regarding threats to the well-being of GLB adolescents. Given how few had come out during high school in this study, attention to affective concerns of *all* gifted students (and all *students*) in small-group discussion (cf. Peterson, 1990) can help to build a supportive climate for expressing developmental concerns. Visible literature related to GLB concerns in counseling or gifted-program offices might also be helpful.

Essentially, short- and long-term policies and strategies intended to move the general school climate toward acceptance and support of GLB students are crucial. It is certainly important to recognize that proactive stances by educators often involve risk for them in terms of response from school constituencies. According to this study, however, inaction may be life-threatening for GLB students. Courageous educators are needed to create a safer climate in schools. Participants' practical suggestions, for example, regarding teachers' squelching of homophobic comments in the classroom and acknowledging the sexual orientation of GLB literary and historical figures represent important directions in this regard. Even in contexts where open advocacy is perceived to be dangerous, following the participants' admonitions may not only be possible, but also important in creating a school climate of safety, compassion, and appreciation for diversity. Curricular and other formal instruction, using either or both cognitive and affective approaches, has also been recommended (e.g., Butler, 1994; Sears, 1991).

LIMITATIONS AND CONCLUSIONS

It is possible that those who had had successful counseling experiences and who were confident in their ability to express their thoughts were most likely to participate in this study, especially given the length and nature of the questionnaire. The number of participants is small, with only one-third of them female. They were also all "out" enough to have received the questionnaire through a university support group, and involvement in such a group may make the findings here nonrepresentative of GLB young adults in general. All of these factors limit the ability to generalize from these findings. It should be noted, however, that these findings, the result of a postpositivistic mode of inquiry, are not necessarily meant to reflect beyond these particular participants. The "task is exploration—and sometimes discovery—of emerging structures" Glasser & Strauss, 1967). The findings here certainly underscore the presence, needs, and concerns of these self-identified gifted GLB adolescents and offer areas for further exploration. In addition, the findings "can be used to speak to or to help form a judgment about other situations" (Eisner & Peshkin, 1990), in this case, other GLB adolescents in other locations.

The participants themselves specifically indicated several topics worthy of further study when asked what questions should have been included on the questionnaire. Substance abuse among GLB adolescents, dropping out of school, the first sexual experience, and the role of the church in coming out were cited as areas about which these high-ability GLB individuals wished they had been asked to comment. It is unknown whether the respondents were simply curious about these topics, already knew these areas were significant concerns among GLB individuals, or wanted educators to be informed about these concerns. Regardless, these areas represent potential research areas regarding gifted GLB adolescents, including dropping out, given the fact that two here had dropped out of high school and others had contemplated it.

These high-ability participants expressed a need for information as adolescents—about sexual development, homosexuality, health concerns, depression, and the complex coming-out process. They needed discussion. The high incidence of depression and suicidal ideation and the fact that few parents and no teachers were informed about these subjects point to a need for attention to affective concerns in gifted programs, including enough discussion of sexual orientation to indicate that it is at least a topic worthy of discussion. Almost all participants reported a sense of alienation and isolation at some point. Many mentioned not knowing any other GLB individuals during adolescence. There is undoubtedly added danger in perceiving no supportive peer culture—to be "without a place" when affirming sexual orientation or when beginning to differentiate from parents. Future studies can focus on these and other developmental issues. Findings in this study can contribute to increased understanding of gifted GLB youth and enhance educators' ability to help them not only to survive adolescence, but also to have satisfying and interpersonally connected lives during that complex developmental stage.

REFERENCES

Anderson, D. (1987). Family and peer relations of gay adolescents. *Adolescent Psychiatry,* *14,* 162–178.

Baker, S., & Campbell, C. A. (Eds.). (1998). Sexual minority youth and the school counselor: The challenges of a hidden minority [Special Issue]. *Professional School Counseling, 1*(3).

Baldauf, S. (1997, September 29). More schools take up gay-bias issues. *The Christian Science Monitor,* 4.

Bart, M. (1998). Creating a safer school for gay students. *Counseling Today, 41*(3), 26, 36, 39.

Ben-Ari, A. (1995). Coming out: A dialectic of intimacy and privacy. *Families in Society: The Journal of Contemporary Human Services, 76,* 306–314.

Benvenuti, A. C. (1986, November). *Assessing and addressing the special challenge of gay and lesbian students for high school counseling programs*. Paper presented at the 65th Annual Meeting of the California Educational Research Association, San Jose, CA. (ERIC Document Reproduction Service No. ED 279 958)

Bohan, J. S. (1996). Teaching on the edge: The psychology of sexual orientation. *Teaching of Psychology, 24*(1), 27–32.

Borhek, M. V. (1993). *Coming out to parents: A two-way survival guide for lesbians and gay men and their parents*. Cleveland, OH: Pilgrim Press.

Boxer, A. M., & Cohler, B. (1989). The life course of gay and lesbian youth: An immodest proposal for the study of lives. *Journal of Homosexuality, 17*, 315–346.

Bradish, C. (1995). Therapeutic programming for gay and lesbian youth: How experiential education can support an at-risk population. *Journal of Experiential Education, 18*, 91–94.

Bridget, J., & Lucille, S. (1996). Lesbian Youth Support Information Service (LYSIS): Developing a distance support agency for young lesbians. *Journal of Community & Applied Social Psychology, 6*, 355–364.

Butler, K. L. (1994, November). *Prospective teachers' knowledge, attitudes, and behavior regarding gay men and lesbians*. (Technical Report No. 143). Kent State University, OH. (ERIC Document Reproduction Service No. ED 379 251).

Cantwell, M. A. (1997). *Homosexuality: The secret a child dares not tell*. San Rafael, CA: Rafael Press.

Cass, V. C. (1979). Homosexual identity formation: A theoretical model. *Journal of Homosexuality, 4*, 219–235.

Colangelo, N., & Brower, P. (1987). Labeling gifted youngsters: Long-term impact on families. *Gifted Child Quarterly, 31*, 75–78.

Coleman, E., & Remafedi, G. (1989). Gay, lesbian, and bisexual adolescents: A critical challenge to counselors. *Journal of Counseling and Development, 68*, 36–40.

Cornell, D. (1984). *Families of gifted children*. Ann Arbor, MI: UMI Research Press.

Cramer, D. W., & Roach, A. J. (1988). Coming out to Mom and Dad: A study of gay males and their relationships with their parents. *Journal of Homosexuality, 15*, 79–91.

Cranston, K. (1992). HIV education for gay, lesbian, and bisexual youth: Personal risk, personal power, and the community of conscience. *Journal of Homosexuality, 22*, 247–259.

Cross, T. L., Coleman, L. J., & Stewart, R. A. (1995). Psychosocial diversity among gifted adolescents: An exploratory study of two groups. *Roeper Review, 17*, 181–185.

Cross, T. L., Coleman, L. J., & Terharr-Yonkers, M. (1991). The social cognition of gifted adolescents in schools: Managing the stigma of giftedness. *Journal for the Education of the Gifted, 15*, 44–55.

Dahlheimer, D., & Feigal, J. (1991). Gays and lesbians in therapy: Bridging the gap. *The Family Therapy Networker, 15*, 44–53.

deMonteflores, C., & Schultz, S. J. (1978). Coming out: Similarities and differences for lesbians and gay men. *Journal of Social Issues, 34*, 59–72.

Dunham, K. L. (1989). *Educated to be invisible*. (ERIC Document Reproduction Service No. ED 336 676)

Edwards, W. J. (1996). A sociological analysis of an invisible minority group: Male adolescent homosexuals. *Youth & Society, 27*, 334–355.

Eisner, E. W., & Peshkin, A. (1990). *Qualitative inquiry in education: The continuing debate*. New York: Teachers College Press.

Elia, J. P. (1993). Homophobia in the high school: A problem in need of a resolution. *High School Journal, 77,* 177–185.

Evans, N., & Levine, H. (1990). Perspectives on sexual orientation. In L. V. Moore (Ed.), *Evolving theoretical perspectives on students.* San Francisco: Jossey-Bass.

Farrell, D. M. (1989). Suicide among gifted students. *Roeper Review, 11,* 134–139.

Ferguson, W. E. (1981). Gifted adolescents, stress, and life changes. *Adolescence, 16,* 973–985.

Fontaine, J. H. (1998). Evidencing a need: School counselors' experiences with gay and lesbian students. *Professional School Counseling, 1*(3), 8–14.

Fontaine, J. H., & Hammond, N. L. (1996). Counseling issues with gay and lesbian adolescents. *Adolescence, 31,* 817–830.

Friedrichs, T. (1997). Understanding the educational needs of gifted gay and bisexual males. *Counseling & Guidance, 6*(3), 3, 8.

Gibson, P. (1989). Gay male and lesbian suicide. In M. R. Reinleib (Ed.), *Report of the secretary's task force on youth suicide* (pp. 3-110–3-137). Washington, DC: U.S. Government Printing Office. (DHHS Pub. No. 89-1622)

Glasser, B. G., & Strauss, A. L. (1967). *The discovery of grounded theory: Strategies for qualitative research.* New York: Aldine.

Griffin, P. (1994). Homophobia in sport: Addressing the needs of lesbian and gay high school athletes. *High School Journal, 77,* 80–87.

Hammelman, T. L. (1993). Gay and lesbian youth: Contributing factors to serious attempts or considerations of suicide. *Journal of Gay and Lesbian Psychotherapy, 2,* 77–89.

Hanckel, F., & Cunningham, J. (1976). Can young gays find happiness in YA books? *Wilson Library Bulletin, 50,* 528–534. (ERIC Document Reproduction Service No. ED EJ 134 772)

Harbeck, K. M. (1994). Invisible no more: Addressing the needs of gay, lesbian, and bisexual youth and their advocates. *High School Journal, 77,* 169–176.

Hayes, M. L., & Sloat, R. S. (1989). Gifted students at risk for suicide. *Roeper Review, 12,* 102–107.

Herdt, G. (1989). Introduction: Gay and lesbian youth: Emergent identities and cultural scenes at home and abroad. *Journal of Homosexuality, 17,* 1–41.

Hershberger, S. L., Pilkington, N. W., & D'Augelli, A. R. (1997). Predictors of suicide attempts among gay, lesbian, and bisexual youth. *Journal of Adolescent Research, 12,* 477–497.

Hetrick, E. S., & Martin, A. D. (1987). Developmental issues and their resolution for gay and lesbian adolescents. *Journal of Homosexuality, 14,* 25–42.

Hewitt, P. L., Newton, J., Flett, G. L., & Callander, L. (1997). Perfectionism and suicide ideation in adolescent psychiatric patients. *Journal of Child Psychology, 25,* 95–101.

Hodges, E. V., Malone, M. J., & Perry, D. G. (1997). Individual risk and social risk as interacting determinants of victimization in the peer group. *Developmental Psychology, 33,* 1032–1039.

Kinsey, A. C., Pomeroy, W. B., & Martin, C. E. (1948). *Sexual behavior in the human male.* Philadelphia: W. B. Saunders.

Kissen, R. M. (1993). Listening to gay and lesbian teenagers. *Teaching Education, 5*(2), 57–68.

Kottman, T., Lingg, M., & Tisdell, T. (1995). Gay and lesbian adolescents: Implications for Adlerian therapists. *Individual Psychology: Journal of Adlerian Theory, Research & Practice, 51,* 114–128.

Lenhardt, A. M. C. (1997). Disenfranchised grief/Hidden sorry: Implications for the school counselor. *The School Counselor, 44,* 264–270.

Lock, J. (1998). Treatment of homophobia in a gay male adolescent. *American Journal of Psychotherapy, 52,* 202–212.

Lovecky, D. V. (1992). Exploring social and emotional aspects of giftedness in children. *Roeper Review, 15,* 18–24.

Mahoney, A. S. (1998). In search of the gifted identity: From abstract concept to workable counseling constructs. *Roeper Review, 20,* 222–226.

McCarthy, C. J., Brack, C. J., Laygo, R. M., Brack, G., & Orr, D. P. (1997). A theory based on investigation of adolescent risk behavior and concern about AIDS. *The School Counselor. 44,* 185–197.

McClintock, M. K., & Herdt, G. (1996). Rethinking puberty: The development of sexual attraction. *Current Directions in Psychological Science, 5(6),* 178–183.

McFarland, W. P. (1998). Gay, lesbian, and bisexual student suicide. *Professional School Counseling, 1(3),* 26–29.

Omizo, M. M., Omizo, S. A., & Okamoto, C. M. (1998). Gay and lesbian adolescents: A phenomenological study. *Professional School Counseling, 1(3),* 35–37.

Peterson, J. S. (1990). Noon-hour discussion: Dealing with the burdens of capability. *Gifted Child Today, 13(4),* 17–22.

Peterson, J. S. (1999). Gifted—through whose cultural lens? An application of the postpositivistic mode of inquiry. *Journal for the Education of the Gifted, 22,* 354–383.

Piechowski, M. M. (1997). Emotional giftedness: The measure of intrapersonal intelligence. In N. Colangelo & G. A. Davis (Eds.), *Handbook of gifted education* (pp. 366–381). Boston: Allyn and Bacon.

Poppenhagen, M. P., & Qualley, R. M. (1998). Adolescent suicide: Detection, intervention, and prevention. *Professional School Counseling, 1(4),* 30–36.

Ritter, K. Y., & O'Neill, C. W. (1989). Moving through loss: The spiritual journey of gay men and lesbian women. *Journal of Counseling and Development, 68,* 9–15.

Roeper, A. (1997). Sexual development in gifted children. *Counseling & Guidance, 6(3),* 1, 4, 9.

Ross, M. W. (1989). Gay youth in four cultures: A comparative study. *Journal of Homosexuality, 17,* 299–314.

Rotheram-Borus, M. J., Hunter, J., & Rosario, M. (1994). Suicidal behavior and gay-related stress among gay and bisexual male adolescents. *Journal of Adolescent Research, 9,* 498–508.

Savin-Williams, R. C. (1990). Gay and lesbian adolescents. *Marriage and Family Review, 14,* 197–216.

Savin-Williams, R. C. (1994). Verbal and physical abuse as stressors in the lives of lesbian, gay male, and bisexual youths: Associations with school problems, running away, substance abuse, prostitution, and suicide. *Journal of Consulting & Clinical Psychology, 62,* 261–269.

Schneider, M. (1989). Sappho was a right-on adolescent: Growing up lesbian. *Journal of Homosexuality, 17,* 111–130.

Schneider, M. S., & Tremble, B. (1986). Training service providers to work with gay or lesbian adolescents: A workshop. *Journal of Counseling & Development, 65,* 98–99.

Schwartz, W. (1994). Improving the school experience for gay, lesbian, and bisexual students. Washington, DC: Office of Educational Research and Improvement. (ERIC Document Reproduction Service No. ED 377 257)

Sears, J. T. (1991). Depicting the fluidity of sexual behavior and identities. *Education Digest, 57(4),* 53–55.

Singerline, H. (1994). OutRight: Reflections on an out-of-school gay youth group. *High School Journal, 77,* 133–137.

Sowa, C. J., & May, K. M. (1997). Expanding Lazarus and Folkman's paradigm to the social and emotional adjustment of gifted children and adolescents (SEAM). *Gifted Child Quarterly, 41*, 36–43.

Sullivan, T., & Schneider, M. (1987). Development and identity issues in adolescent homosexuality. *Child and Adolescent Social Work, 4*(1), 13–24.

Sumara, D. (1993). Telling tales of surprise. In W. F. Pinar (Ed.), *Queer theory in education* (pp. 197–219). Mahwah, NJ: Erlbaum.

Tolan, S. S. (1997). Sex and the highly gifted adolescent. *Counseling & Guidance, 6*(3), 2, 5, 8.

Uribe, V. (1994). The silent minority: Rethinking our commitment to gay and lesbian youth. *Theory into Practice, 33*, 167–172.

Uribe, V., & Harbeck, K. M. (1992). Addressing the needs of lesbian, gay, and bisexual youth: The origins of project 10 and school-based intervention. *Journal of Homosexuality, 22*, 9–27.

Waldner-Haugrud, L. K., & Magruder, B. (1996). Homosexual identity expression among lesbian and gay adolescents. *Youth & Society, 27*, 313–333.

Webb, J. T., Meckstroth, E. A., & Tolan, S. S. (1982). *Guiding the gifted child: A practical source for parents and teachers.* Dayton, OH: Ohio Psychology Press.

Weisse, D. E. (1990). Gifted adolescents and suicide. *The School Counselor, 37*, 351–358.

Zera, D. (1992). Coming of age in a heterosexist world: The development of gay and lesbian adolescents. *Adolescence, 27*, 849–854.

Appendix

Questionnaire Items (presented here in an altered format)

Age_____ Gender_____ Years of Formal Education_____
Current Status re: Career/Job/School
_____

1. What was your experience during grades 5–8 in school socially?
    emotionally?
    academically?
    What was your experience during grades 9–12 in school socially?
    emotionally?
    academically?
    Were you identified as "gifted"?

2. When did you begin to wonder about your sexual orientation?
    What led you to wonder about your sexual orientation?
    Did you talk with anyone about this when you first wondered about it?
    If yes, with whom? If yes, what was his/her response?
    Did your wondering about this affect your life at this point?
    If yes, how?

3. When were you convinced that you were gay/lesbian/bisexual?
    Did that realization affect your life at school? If yes, in what way(s)?
    Did it affect your life at home? If yes, in what way(s)?
    Did it affect your relationship with your mother? If yes, in what way(s)?
    With your father? If yes, in what way(s)?
    With your peers? If yes, in what way(s)?
    With your best friend(s)? If yes, in what way(s)?
    Did you ever feel in danger because of your sexual orientation?
    If yes, in what circumstances?
    What were some classroom or school extra-curricular experiences that you associate with your sexual orientation, positively or negatively (for example, as offering support, as contributing to discomfort, as seeming inappropriate, as helpful)?

4. Do you believe you (have) developed coping strategies to help you in regard to living as a gay/lesbian/bisexual during adolescence (and/or later in your life)? If yes, please cite.

5. Have you had any counseling at any time?
    If yes, when?
    If yes, for how long?
    If you had counseling, was it helpful? If yes, what was helpful?
    If you had counseling, did you discuss your sexual orientation with the counselor?
    If you discussed sexual orientation, what was the general approach/attitude of the counselor in this regard?
    Do you have any suggestions as to how the counselor could have been more helpful?

6. When (if ever) did you "come out" to family?
    What were (have been) their reaction(s)?
    When (if ever) did you "come out" to friends?
    What were (have been) their reactions?
    Who (of family, friends) has been supportive?

7. Some theorists have claimed that gifted individuals are hypersensitive to their environment, to feelings, to relationships, and to success/failure/transitions losses/change.
    If those theorists are correct, what kind of impact might that hypersensitivity have had on your experience as a gay person during your school years? (If you don't support these theorists' view, simply ignore this question.)
    Do you believe your high ability has created particular (relative to the rest of the population) needs for you, especially as a gay person? If yes, in what ways?
    How have you used your intelligence (intellect, social intelligence, etc.) to enhance your life and/or relate to society as a gay person?

8. Did you experience (have you experienced) depression during your school years?
    If yes, for how long?
    If yes, did you ever discuss those feelings with anyone?
    If yes, with whom?
    Did you ever consider suicide?
    If yes, when?
    If yes, did you ever discuss those thoughts with anyone?
    If yes, with whom?

Continued

If you experienced "low" times, what strategies were helpful in coping with them?

9. Do/Did you attend college?

If yes, what were (have been) some of your experiences during that time in regard to gaining self-understanding, finding support, finding a niche in life, finding direction, etc.?

If you have attended college, has your college experience been (was your experience) mostly positive or mostly negative socially? Academically?

10. What do you wish your elementary, middle school, or high school teachers/coaches/administrators had understood about you?

In general, what do you think educators and counselors should understand about the school experiences of adolescents who are gay/lesbian/bisexual?

What would have helped your precollege school experiences, in regard to sexual-orientation issues and concerns?

What kind of information and training do you think educators should have in order to be what gay adolescents need them to be?

11. Do you think gifted education should focus (at least to some extent, e.g., in individual sessions) specifically on the "gifted and gay" theme at conferences for educators?

If yes, why? (If not, why not?)

12. Have you been able to have satisfying, stable relationships since high school?

13. What questions do you think should have been part of this questionnaire and weren't—i.e., what are some concerns (particularly related to the adolescent/young-adult experience) about which you wish someone would ask?

Additional thoughts, concerns, feedback:

7

The Rural Gifted Child

Howard H. Spicker

Indiana University

W. Thomas Southern

Bowling Green State University

Beverly I. Davis

Katy, Texas

The effects of such characteristics as rural living, sparse population, poverty, non-urban acculturation experiences, and traditional rural values are related to the difficulties in providing for the educational needs of rural gifted students. Some promising solutions to these problems are suggested. Included are non-traditional identification procedures, computer and video linkages between school systems, cooperative personnel development, and sharing of special service staffs for the gifted.

Editor's Note: From Spicker, H. H., Southern, W. T., & Davis, B. I. (1987). The rural gifted child. *Gifted Child Quarterly*, *31*(4), 155-157. © 1987 National Association for Gifted Children. Reprinted with permission.

M any people believe that because of improved transportation and instant communication, rural America is no longer distinguishable from urban America (Friedman & Miller, 1965). Others believe that with the near elimination of the one-room school and the consolidation of American school districts from approximately 118,000 in 1940 to 16,000 in 1978, traditional rural education no longer exists (Carmichael, 1982).

The purpose of this paper is to show that despite the consolidation of our schools, traditional rural values, characteristics, and beliefs are very much alive and continue to have a profound influence on rural education in general and on the education of rural gifted children in particular. It is only when these rural educational influences are understood that one can isolate the problems they produce and then attempt to solve them.

What is meant by the term rural? Governmental agencies define rural on the basis of population, and use population figures that range from less than 2,500 according to the Census Bureau (U.S. Department of Commerce, 1982) to less than 50,000 according to the Rural Development Act of 1972 loan application criteria. However, rural America is far too complex to be defined by population alone. As stated by Mathews (1982), "The key to definition is not in numbers but in the relationships between people and between people and the land" (p. 1627). Rural education, then, is the interaction of the characteristics of sparsely populated communities with the traditional rural values and beliefs of their inhabitants. These include belief in free public education, primacy of local control, smallness of the school, inadequate school finances, and, in many instances, poor economic status of its residents (Carmichael, 1982). Because of these characteristics "rural schools tend to 1) offer a more limited curriculum than metropolitan schools, 2) offer fewer libraries and fewer programs for special populations, and 3) employ fewer support personnel such as counselors and curriculum specialists." (Carmichael, 1982, p. 6). Despite these shortcomings, a recent Gallup poll and a 1979 survey by the Department of Housing and Urban Development showed that rural people are generally pleased with their schools (Lewis, 1982).

The characteristics of traditional rural schools and the general satisfaction of rural people with their schools pose special problems for the education of rural gifted children. Among, the more prevailing problems are small community size, poverty, and non-urban acculturation. The relationship of these problems to the education of gifted students must be understood if we are to provide adequate educational services to those students.

THE PROBLEM OF SIZE

Two-thirds of the nation's school districts have enrollments of less than 2,500 students (Lewis, 1982). A gifted prevalence of 5% applied to that figure would identify 125 or fewer gifted students in two-thirds of our school districts. When these small numbers are further divided by twelve or thirteen grades, the five federally recognized categories of giftedness, and the typical wide range that encompasses the abilities of gifted students, it becomes readily apparent why providing appropriate educational programs for these small numbers of gifted students becomes a major undertaking.

THE PROBLEM OF POVERTY

Of the 250 poorest counties in the nation, comprising 40% of the poor in the United States, all are rural and 237 are in the South. Of all blacks living outside metropolitan areas, 41% have incomes below the poverty level and almost all live in the South (Lewis, 1982). Similar rural impoverishment is found among Mexican-Americans in the Southwest, Native Americans in the West, and among poor whites in Appalachia. The characteristics of children from impoverished backgrounds reviewed by Michael and Dodson (1978) include a deficiency in language skills, lack of perceptual skill development in language differentiation, lack of stimulation for asking or answering questions, lack of enrichment activities, lack of concern over school attendance, lack of curiosity due to paucity of objects in the home, lack of support by parents of the school establishment, lack of parental understanding of the educative process, lack of quiet time for fostering discriminatory listening skills, lack of self-confidence, lack of time consciousness, and lack of vocabulary related to the school establishment. Students of high potential from such impoverished backgrounds require special identification, motivational, and instructional procedures as well as innovative curriculum modifications if they are to attain their intellectual and creative potential.

THE PROBLEM OF NON–URBAN ACCULTURATION IN IDENTIFICATION

Standardized intelligence and achievement tests assume that subjects taking the tests have been exposed to comparable acculturation experiences (Newland, 1980). It is quite evident that the rural children of Mexican-American migrant workers, southern black sharecroppers, native American reservation Indians, and Appalachian mountain people have experiences far different from those of urban children. It has been well documented that these social and cultural differences result in IQ scores that are ten to fifteen points below those of advantaged, middle class children (Mercer, 1973). Less well-known are the experiential deficits of traditional white rural children. For example, the mean IQs obtained by Terman and Merrill's (1937) urban and rural standardization samples were 105.7 and 99.2 respectively. Even more interesting was the mean IQ drop of seven points by rural children after the preschool period. Although Terman and Merrill hypothesized that "the lowered IQ of rural children may be ascribed to the relatively poorer educational facilities in rural communities"

(p. 49), it is equally possible that the test items favored the acculturation experiences of urban children. The recent revision of the Stanford-Binet (Thorndike, Hagan, & Sattler, 1986) reveals a reversal of that rural-urban difference, with rural children exceeding the mean IQ of urban children by more than five points.

Despite the increased urbanization of many of our rural children, there remains a subclass of high potential rural students who exhibit behaviors that are antithetical to those of typical gifted students. These include speaking in a non-standard English regional dialect, being less verbal in their oral language communications, having limited experiences outside the community in which they reside, and being relatively unaffected by the pressures of time. These children may constitute 20% or more of the enrollments of a rural consolidated school corporation.

OTHER PROBLEMS ASSOCIATED WITH RURAL GIFTED EDUCATION

1. The acceptance of the status quo and resistance to change make it difficult to initiate new offerings for the special needs of gifted students. The parental group pressures that provide the impetus for starting gifted and talented programs in urban and suburban schools are much less likely to be found in rural schools.

2. The average spending of rural school districts is about 20% less per pupil than that of metropolitan school districts (Lewis, 1982). This tenuous economic support base precludes extensive or expensive program additions, particularly when it may be perceived that such programs will benefit only a small select number of students.

3. The small, less specialized teaching staffs of rural secondary schools and their large number of preparations across many different subjects make it difficult for them to keep up with curriculum developments in all subjects. This lack of content specialization is likely to deny gifted students access to specialized and up-to-date content knowledge (Dunn, 1977).

4. Highly trained teachers, particularly in the various support areas, are few in number and tend to use rural school districts as temporary stepping stones in their career ladder (Dunne, 1977). Hence there are fewer counselors, school psychologists, psychometrists, and curriculum specialists to assist the faculty in building adequate programs for the gifted.

5. The inwardness and self-sufficiency indicated by the belief in the primacy of local control make it less likely that such districts will seek outside assistance from state agencies or universities in efforts to serve the needs of gifted students.

PROMISING SOLUTIONS

Despite the magnitude of the problems involved in providing programs for rural gifted and talented populations, some potential solutions are available. To establish effective rural gifted programs, it is crucial to include opportunities for the traditional rural as well as the urban acculturated middle and professional middle class students that constitute the enrollments of many of today's consolidated rural school districts. This requires selection procedures that are bias fair to the characteristics of traditional rural children.

Identification of gifted populations in rural areas should therefore include non-traditional screening and selection procedures. Promising formal testing procedures include the use of untimed, non-verbal intelligence tests with measures of spatial abilities. Informal procedures might include analysis of student products (writings, collections, projects) and anecdotal information obtained from teachers and parents. Efforts should be made to compare students on their ability to solve problems outside the constraints of standardized tests. Teachers responsible for identifying gifted students require intensive inservice training to make them aware of prejudices they may harbor in evaluating certain students. These include language and behavioral differences of students from lower socio-economic minority ethnic backgrounds. Biases against non-standard English dialects and grammatically incorrect writing are particularly difficult to change. Moreover, teachers should be made aware that knowledge of the home and background of their students is a two-edged sword. While it can amplify the information they have about each student, it may also interfere with unbiased assessment of those students known to come from psychosocially deprived homes.

The often fierce competition between neighboring communities requires that the program be tailored to the perceived uniqueness of each school district. The pride and closeness of the rural community can be harnessed by involving the community in the educational effort. The training and use of local people for program staff, the reliance on developing local mentors and community resources, and the integration of themes of local importance into the curriculum can appeal to the sense of pride and local ownership that will help insure acceptance. It is also important to emphasize that the talents of gifted children, if properly nurtured, can help solve the community's problems and meet the needs of the future. If that resource is not challenged and developed, it will be dissipated, much to the detriment of the community.

Sparsity of population and paucity of fiscal and community resources can be addressed if rural districts are willing to share their strengths with one another. Adjacent districts can cooperate in several ways.

1. They can share personnel and the financial burdens for planning and conducting staff development and inservice training activities.

2. Certified teachers and special service staffs for the gifted can be shared in the same manner as handicapped programs are presently shared in many rural districts through special educational cooperatives.

3. Students can be bused across district lines for pull-out programs, college credit classes, and even advanced high school courses offered in one district but not another.

Linkages may even be extended beyond adjacent school districts. Modern technology has been harnessed to provide satellite television instruction and video hook-ups to isolated schools for many years. Micro-computers and telecommunication networks can be used to forge linkages between widely separated districts. Those linkages carry a number of benefits:

1. Teachers in specialized disciplines can exchange lesson plans and teaching resources.

2. Gifted students can interact with one another for social and educational exchanges.

3. Gifted students and their teachers can obtain locally unavailable information from information exchange centers, library search services, and even university content experts.

The efficacy of such a micro-computer and audio/video tape exchange network for rural school corporations was investigated by Spicker and Southern (1985). Approximately 125 gifted middle school students and their teachers from six geographically separated school corporations were linked together by a computer bulletin board maintained at Indiana University. The information exchange focused around two common instructional units. One dealt with the study of environmental problems unique to each community (e.g. strip mining, soil reclamation, dune erosion, river pollution, and wetland wildlife sanctuaries) and the other with the impact of various immigrant groups on the development of each community. Both units were community focused to capitalize on the local pride common to most rural towns. The projects permitted information exchanges between students across the six sites, provided information retrieval from the university library and faculty consultants, and presented opportunities for social interactions with students who had similar abilities and interests.

As the technology becomes less expensive and more widely available, the opportunities for rural districts to initiate and participate in such projects will grow. If the concept of cooperation can be made palatable, many of the obstacles occasioned by small size can be alleviated.

SUMMARY AND CONCLUSIONS

It is evident from this review that an effort should be made to separate the rural effects on student learning from those of ethnicity and poverty. Because the research to date has concentrated on the effects of impoverishment and ethnic origin the true impact of rural isolation and traditional rural values has yet to be calculated.

Special procedures for identifying traditional, less verbal rural gifted students need to be found; social interaction opportunities for moderately and highly gifted students should be provided; cultural, intellectual, and scientific resources should be made accessible. Once solutions to these special problems are found, the needs of rural gifted children will at last be served.

REFERENCES

Carmichael, D. (1982) The challenge of rural education. *The Rural Educator* 4(1), 5–10.

Dunne, F. (1977) Choosing smallness: An examination of the small school experience in rural America. In J. P. Sher (Ed.), *Education in rural America*. Boulder, CO: Westview Press, 81–124.

Fratoe, F. A. (1978) Rural education and rural labor force in the seventies. *Rural Development Research Report No. 5*, Washington D.C.: U.S. Department of Agriculture.

Friedman, J., & Miller, J. (1965) The urban field. *Journal of the American Institute of Planners, 31*, 312–320.

Lewis, A. (1982) *Ensuring excellence in rural education.* Proceedings of the rural education seminar. Washington D.C.: American Association of School Administrators.

Mathews, W. F. (1982) Rural education. *Encyclopedia of education research.* New York: The Free Press.

Mercer, J. R. (1973*) Labeling the mentally retarded.* Berkeley: University of California Press.

Michael, B. M., & Dodson, E. (1978) *SPICE workshop model:* An approach to alternative programs for the disadvantaged gifted. ED 164478.

Nachtigal, P. M. (1982) Education in rural America: An overview. In P.M. Nachtigal (Ed.), *Rural education in search of a better way.* Boulder, CO: Westview Press, 3–13.

Newland, T. E. (1980) Psychological assessment of exceptional children and youth. In W. H. Cruickshank (Ed.), *Psychology of exceptional children and youth:* Fourth edition. Englewood Cliffs, NJ: Prentice-Hall, 115–172.

Peterson, B. (1974) Getting back to our roots. *Life in rural America.* Washington D.C.: *National Geographic Society.*

Spicker, H. H., & Southern, W. T. (1985). Indiana University's rural information network for the gifted (Project R.I.N.G.). Paper presented at the 6th World Conference on Gifted and Talented Children, Hamburg, West Germany.

Terman, L. M., & Merrill, M. A. (1937) *Measuring intelligence.* Boston: Houghton Mifflin.

Thorndike, R. L., Hagan, E. P., & Sattler, J. M. (1986) The Stanford-Binet intelligence scale: Fourth edition, *Technical Manual.* Chicago: Riverside.

U.S. Department of Commerce, Bureau of the Census. (1982) *1980 Census of the population. General population characteristics.* Washington, D.C.: U.S. Government Printing Office.

8

Gifted Dropouts: The Who and the Why

Joseph S. Renzulli

Sunghee Park

The University of Connecticut

Two studies were conducted to obtain comprehensive information about gifted high school dropouts and to examine factors that are related to their dropout behavior using the Dropout and Student questionnaires of the National Education Longitudinal Study of 1988 (NELS:88). The results indicated that many gifted dropouts were from low socioeconomic-status families and racial minority groups; had parents with low levels of education; and participated less in extracurricular activities. Also, reasons for gifted male dropouts were more related to economic issues, while reasons for gifted female dropouts were more related to personal issues, although both males and females were likely to offer school-related reasons. The

Editor's Note: From Renzulli, J. S., & Park, S. (2000). Gifted dropouts: The who and the why. *Gifted Child Quarterly*, 44(4), 261-271. © 2000 National Association for Gifted Children. Reprinted with permission.

logistic regression analysis results indicated that dropout behavior for gifted students was significantly related to students' educational aspirations, pregnancy or child-rearing, gender, father's highest level of education, and mother's highest level of education.

Gifted dropouts appear on a self-actualizing quest; the wander-lust is a means to an end that may not be fully understood, but is an affective and a cognitive component of identity, development as they strive for their niche in the world.

—Elsie Robertson (1991, p. 67)

The problem of high school dropouts has generated increased interest from researchers, educators, and policy makers. The recent report by the National Center for Education Statistics (NCES, 1997) reported that, each year, approximately 300,000 to 500,000 students left high school without completing their programs. For example, in 1996, 3.6 million youths, who comprised 11.1% of the 32.4 million 16- through 24-year-olds in the U.S., were not enrolled in a high school program and had not completed high school. This report also indicated that dropout rates varied significantly by racial background and socioeconomic status. Although the gap between the rates for Blacks and Whites narrowed, dropout rates for Hispanics remained higher than those for White and Black students. Students from the lowest income families were approximately eight times more likely to be dropouts than those from the highest income families (NCES, 1997).

Although the issue of high school dropouts has received much attention, only limited research has been devoted to gifted or high-ability dropouts (Robertson, 1991; Sadowski, 1987; Stephenson, 1985), and little is known about these students. In fact, a wide range of estimates exists for the percentage of gifted students who drop out of school. Robertson reported that 25% of all students who drop out of school do so by age 16, and between 18% and 250% of gifted and talented students drop out. *U.S. News & World Report* reported in August, 1983 that up to 18% of all high school dropouts are gifted students (Solorzano, 1983). The Marland Report (cited by Irvine, 1987) stated that 18% of dropouts are gifted. However, Irvine criticized this finding: "We don't know how many gifted students drop out, but it's not 18 percent. The Marland Report (1972) was incorrectly interpreted that approximately 18 percent of high school dropouts are gifted" (p. 79).

Putting the Research to Use

Due to very limited research on gifted dropouts, we do not have much information about this group. What is the major reason that gifted students leave school? How do parents respond to their children's dropout behavior? What are gifted dropout students' personal backgrounds? What factors are related to gifted students' dropout decisions? Studies dealing with these questions are important because they help to provide research-based information for teachers, parents, counselors, and policy makers. Findings of this study indicate that schools and teachers should communicate closely with the parents of potential gifted dropouts. Parents should have more involvement in their children's personal and school-related problems; and counseling services that focus on dropout prevention should be targeted at culturally diverse, minority, and economically disadvantaged gifted students. The findings reported in this article can serve as the basis for developing guidelines for targeting potential dropouts, developing appropriate curricula, and developing challenging programs for potential gifted dropouts.

This variation in gifted dropout estimates is partly due to the multiple definitions of giftedness. In fact, the previous studies about gifted dropouts have focused on academically high-ability students, selected primarily by IQ score. However, recent trends for defining gifted and talented have become broad and flexible. In his three-ring conception of giftedness, Renzulli (1986) argued that there is no single criterion for giftedness. Rather, interaction among the three clusters of traits including above-average, though not necessarily superior, ability; task commitment; and creativity contribute to the development of gifted behaviors. According to this theory, nonintellective factors like motivation are also important and should be considered. The federal Javits Gifted and Talented Students Education Act defined children with outstanding talent in the following ways, supporting the broad definition of gifted:

> Children and youth with outstanding talent perform or show the potential for performing at remarkably high levels of accomplishment when compared with others of their age, experience, or environment. These children and youth exhibit high performance capability in intellectual, creative, and/or artistic areas, possess an unusual leadership capacity, or excel in specific academic fields. They require services or activities not ordinarily provided by the schools. (U.S. Department of Education, 1993, p. 26)

As Lajoie and Shore (1981) indicated, a study of school dropouts that includes a broad definition of giftedness may achieve different results from a study with a restricted definition, but it is unclear how they might differ.

Another issue in the study of gifted dropouts is the difficulty in obtaining longitudinal data about this population (Robertson, 1991). Although various research studies have been proposed for studying high school dropouts, Kunkel and his colleagues (1991) indicated that previous research studies have not clarified the process of dropping out because they examined only a few variables, such as student or institutional characteristics. Willett and Singer (1991) also noted that research should study a single cohort of students for several years, instead of several cohorts of students for a single year. Tinto (1975, 1982, 1988) argued that attrition is a process that occurs over time, rather than a discrete event that is isolated from other experiences of the student (Kunkel et al., 1991). Bachman, Green, and Wirtinen (1972) also indicated that the dropout decision is long in the making and is based on the student's persona/background, traits, abilities, and school experiences. It is obvious that longitudinal data for gifted dropouts are necessary; however, it is not easy to gather these types of data. As Robertson indicated, a high percentage of gifted dropouts have the ability to graduate from high school and continue further levels of education, and this group presents a major loss of potential to self and society. There is, however, very limited research about this group.

REVIEW OF THE LITERATURE

Factors Related to High School Dropouts

Students' personal backgrounds, including sex, race, socioeconomic status, family background, and personal problems, have been considered to affect students' decisions to drop out of high school (Beacham, 1980; Bernoff, 1981; Curtis, McDonald, Doss, & Davis, 1983; Noth & O'Neill, 1981; Young & Reich, 1974). Studying eighth graders and high school students in Dade County, Stephenson (1985) found that almost 60% of the dropping out took place during the first two years of high school, and Blacks were likely to drop out later than other groups. However, Lobosco (1992) found that, after controlling for family background and other factors, Blacks were more likely to graduate from high school than Whites, Asians, or Hispanics. Similarly, the NCES (1993) report stated that the stereotype of the high school dropout as a Black male is not true. According to the report, the proportion of Black male students leaving school in 1992 was lower than White males (3.3%) and White females (4%), Black females (6.7%), Hispanic males (7.6%), and Hispanic females (9%). Bracey (1994) indicated that, "When differences in the relative sizes of the groups are factored in, the picture of the typical dropout is that of a White, middle-income student." Whites account for 59% of all dropouts, and students from middle-income families account for 57% (NCES).

Many research studies have specified that family factors are significantly related to the decision of students to drop out. Studies found that the dropout's family was less solid, less influenced by a father, less likely to interact in leisure activities, and less able to communicate than the persister's family (Noth & O'Neill, 1981; Sadowski, 1987). Research studies also indicated that loss of a family member due to death or divorce and other family problems influence a student's decision to drop out (Martin, 1981; Massey & Crosby, 1982; Rumberger, 1981). In addition, the level of education and the occupation of dropouts' parents were significant factors in several studies (Martin, 1981; Noth & O'Neill, 1981; Watson, 1976). Other studies acknowledged personal circumstances to be significant in determining the characteristics of high school dropouts: behavior problems (Beacham, 1980; Curtis et al., 1983; Massey & Crosby, 1982); need or preference to work (Noth & O'Neill, 1981; Young & Reich, 1974); low grade-point average (Beacham, 1980; NCES, 1983); and marriage and pregnancy (NCES).

The literature has also suggested that some academic factors, such as low grade-point average, absence, academic failure, lack of interest in school, and dislike for school and teachers, are related to the decision to drop out (Beacham, 1980; Cervantes, 1965; Curtis et al., 1983; Hewitt & Johnson, 1979; Martin, 1981; Massey & Crosby, 1982; NCES, 1983; Noth & O' Neill, 1981; Rumberger, 1981; Schreiber, 1979; Sewell, Palmo, & Manni, 1981; Thornburg, 1975; Young & Reich, 1974).

Beacham (1980) indicated that lack of interest in school is one of the major reasons for dropping out. Similar results were found by Barr and Knowles (1986), who reported that school experiences were important influences in a student's decision to leave school. These students perceive schools as uninteresting and boring places that do not provide challenges. Using discriminant function analysis, Frazer (1992) found that four variables were significant in classifying dropouts: grade-point average, being older than other students, being new to the system, and the number of days that the student attended eighth grade. Soltys (1990) also indicated that absenteeism, lower grade-point averages, and higher rates of school suspensions were significant predictors of students' dropping out. On the other hand, Cordy (1993) reported that the presence of a caring adult, a supportive peer group, alternative educational programs, academic success, motivation to attend postsecondary educational institutions, and participation in fundamental religious groups were reasons at-risk students chose to stay in school rather than drop out. Hertz (1989) argued that educators who accommodate a variety of learning styles can also be a positive factor. Roderick (1991) found that dropout rates increased after transition periods, such as moving from one school to another. She also found that, even after controlling for background and school performance, students who had repeated grades were substantially more likely to drop out regardless of when the grade retention had occurred. Sewell, Palmo, and Manni (1981) indicated that the poor academic performance and dropout behavior might result primarily from the failure to keep up with school curriculum:

> However, the discrepancy between the intellectual potential and the poor achievement among dropouts suggests that if academic failure

which restricts promotion and increases alienation from school is a major factor in early school leaving, factors other than IQ such as achievement motivation, social class influence, and the institutional impact of the school must be further explored to identify the possible reasons for academic failure. (p. 73)

Focusing on gifted dropouts, Robertson (1991) also emphasized school-related factors, such as schools' failure to address the needs of gifted students and their learning styles. She indicated that schools may not present curricula that address the appropriate learning styles of gifted students. As proof, she indicated that biographies of scientists, writers, performers in the visual and performing arts, business magnates, and athletes reveal that many of them dropped out of school from the elementary years on through secondary school. She stated:

Gifted children are qualitatively different from others, and those who are potential dropouts are qualitatively different from other gifted children. . . . An important dimension of the culture of a school is respect for self, for others, and for the school environment. . . . Also both gifted and at-risk students are clear when they discuss the irrelevance of the curriculum. . . . It appears that the gifted potential dropout needs the following: an experiential learning process, individual projects of the students' own choice, challenging and difficult problems within the real world, some competition and challenge from others, the ability to make decisions for self regarding what will be learned and how it will be learned. Gifted students who may drop out of school need to work with a teacher who models a consultant role or works as a smart colleague in a mentor relationship. (pp. 69–70)

Although a small percentage of gifted students drop out of high school, Robertson made suggestions for dealing with this group based on qualitative data that may be of value in dealing with potential gifted dropouts.

Characteristics of Gifted Dropouts

Sadowski (1987) found the following characteristics in his case study of gifted high school dropouts: (1) There was evidence of instability in the home environment; (2) drug and alcohol consumption were a part of the dropout's environment; (3) gifted dropouts exhibited a lack of interest and motivation in high school; (4) there was evidence of a negative and rebellious attitude towards school and authority; (5) there was evidence of an incomplete or inappropriate gifted curriculum in high school; (6) gifted dropouts developed poor peer relationships and exhibited poor social adjustment; and (7) there was evidence of lack of counseling in high school and inadequate communication between the school and the home (p. i).

Betts and Neihart (1988) developed profiles of gifted and talented students on the basis of their behavior, feelings, and needs. According to the profiles, gifted and talented dropouts were depressed and withdrawn because their needs and feelings were not addressed. School did not support their talent and interest and seemed irrelevant to them. Indicating that gifted dropouts' self-esteem is very low, Betts and Neihart recommended family counseling and individual counseling to help promote self-esteem.

Although research studies generally indicate that gifted dropouts may show signs of maladjustment, problems with authority, nonconformity, family conflicts, hostility, suspiciousness, oversensitivity, and egotism (Davis, 1984; Johnson, 1970; Vaughan, 1968), others have suggested that high-ability dropouts are not emotionally maladjusted, but have different developmental needs (Robertson, 1991; Zaccaria & Creaser, 1971). Robertson stated that, although the reasons for dropping out appear similar between gifted and nongifted students, the underlying motivation is different (see quote at the beginning of this article). She further commented:

> Non-gifted dropouts are escaping from the hostile academic world, viewing the real world as less inimical to them than school. . . . Gifted dropouts tend to have more supportive families, have more money, come from a value system that encourages self expression and development, are non-minority, and speak English as a primary language. (Robertson, p. 67)

The purpose of this study is to obtain comprehensive information about gifted high school dropouts and to examine factors that are related to gifted students' dropout behavior using nationally representative longitudinal data.

STUDY 1

Research Questions

1. What are gifted dropouts' reasons for leaving school, what are parents' reactions to their leaving school, and what activities account for their time?

2. Is there any difference between gifted dropouts and nongifted dropouts with respect to their plan to return to school?

Research Design and Data

In this study, data were used from the National Education Longitudinal Study of 1988 (NELS:88), which have been collected on a nationally representative sample of students by the National Center for Education Statistics (NCES).

NELS:88 began in 1988 by collecting data on approximately 25,000 eighth-grade students, including data from their parents, teachers, and school administrators. Students completed a self-administered questionnaire and a cognitive test on reading, math, science, and history/citizenship/geography (NCES, 1994a). In the first follow-up (1990), students also completed a questionnaire and a cognitive test. In addition to this student questionnaire, a dropout questionnaire was given to students who had dropped out of school at some point between the spring term of the 1987–88 school year and that of the 1989–90 school year. The second follow-up data, collected in 1992, included the same components as the first follow-up, plus the parents' questionnaire, students' transcripts, and course offering information. In the second follow-up, a dropout questionnaire was given to the students who had dropped out of school at some point between the spring term of the 1987-88 school year and the spring term of the 1991-92 school year. The questionnaire covered reasons for leaving school, school experiences, absenteeism, plans for the future, employment, attitudes and self-concept, and home environment. Data from the third follow-up were collected in 1994, two years after the students graduated (see NCES, 1994a).

Two studies were conducted using two different sources of data and samples. In Study 1, the Second Follow-Up Dropout questionnaire of NELS:88 was directly analyzed to get more specific information about gifted dropout students. Because only dropout students completed this questionnaire, gifted dropout and nongifted dropout students were compared. In Study 2, student questionnaire data from the base year, the second follow-up, and the third follow-up were analyzed to examine personal and educational factors that are related to decisions to drop out of school by gifted students. Because the NELS:88 data were collected using stratified cluster sampling, some groups of students were oversampled (Keith & Benson, 1992). Therefore, to obtain an accurate estimate, variables must be weighted with an appropriate weight variable to compensate for unequal probabilities of selection and adjusted for the nonresponse effect. In this study, a panel weight was used to compensate for this. Also, in NELS:88, the sampling error overstates the precision of test statistics in the data analyses because of the nature of the complex sample design. The SUDAAN (Software for Statistical Analysis of Correlated Data) statistical program from the Research Triangle Institute (1995) was used to estimate the standard errors, taking into account the complex survey design in both Study 1 and Study 2.

Sample of the Study

The sample of Study 1 consists of dropout students who were not in an academic program leading to a high school diploma, had not received a GED by the spring of 1992, and who completed the dropout questionnaire in the second follow-up. In this study, to apply a more flexible definition of gifted, gifted students were defined as those who participated in their school district's gifted programs or who had been enrolled in three or more classes in advanced,

Table I   Numbers and Percentages of Gifted Male and Female Dropouts Who Reported Various Reasons for Dropping Out of School

Reasons for Leaving School	Gifted Male Dropouts		Gifted Female Dropouts	
	n = 173	%	n = 161	%
I got a job.	66	40.7	30	19.7
I didn't like school.	61	37.4	54	35.5
I couldn't get along with teachers.	48	29.6	24	15.9
I couldn't get along with other students.	22	13.8	24	15.9
I wanted to have a family.	13	8.1	19	12.6
I was pregnant.	—	—	51	33.8
I became a parent.	20	12.6	44	29.1
I had to support my family.	26	16.4	29	19.1
I was suspended from school.	35	22.2	10	6.6
I did not feel safe at school.	18	11.3	14	9.3
I wanted to travel.	10	6.3	10	6.6
My friends had dropped out of school.	18	11.4	6	2.0
I had to care for a family member.	19	12.0	16	10.6
I was expelled from school.	28	17.7	9	6.0
I felt I didn't belong at school.	34	21.3	32	21.1
I couldn't keep up with my schoolwork.	61	38.1	35	23.2
I was failing school.	77	49.0	44	29.1
I got married or planned to get married.	11	6.9	32	21.1
I changed schools and didn't like the new school.	20	12.7	15	10.1
I couldn't work and go to school at same time.	52	32.7	22	14.6
I had a drug/alcohol problem.	12	7.6	3	2.0
I had another problem.	31	26.7	34	26.8

Note: Sum of the percentage is not equal to 100 because dropouts responded either "yes" or "no" on each item. N = 334.

enriched, or accelerated English, social studies, science, or math. Among 1,285 students who completed the second follow-up dropout questionnaire, 334 were identified as gifted.

DATA ANALYSES AND RESULTS

Research Question 1

Several descriptive data analyses were conducted to gain specific information about gifted dropouts who completed the second follow-up dropout questionnaire regarding: (1) reasons for leaving school; (2) parents' reactions; (3) time that gifted dropouts spent using computers, not including playing video/computer games; (4) time that gifted dropouts spent working on hobbies, arts, or crafts on their own; and (5) time that gifted dropouts spent doing volunteer work or community services.

Regarding reasons for leaving school, gifted dropouts were asked to respond to 22 items, saying whether the items were related to their decision to drop out. The results indicated that the majority of the gifted male dropouts left school because: (1) I was failing school (49.0%), (2) I got a job (40.7%), (3) I couldn't keep up with my schoolwork (38.1%), (4) I didn't like school (37.4%), and (5) I couldn't work and go to school at the same time (32.7%). The reasons for leaving school by gifted male dropouts were mainly school-related and job-related, while the reasons reported by gifted female dropouts were more related to personal and school problems. Gifted female dropouts reported that they left school because: (1) I didn't like school (35.5%), (2) I was pregnant (33.8%), (3) I became a parent (29.1%) and I was failing school (29.1%), (4) I had another problem (26.8%), and (5) I couldn't keep up with my schoolwork (23.2%). In both groups, school-related reasons such as "I did not like school" and "I am failing school" were main reasons for leaving school (see Table 1).

The examination of the dropouts' reports of their parents' reaction to the dropout behavior revealed that many of the dropouts' parents (75%) tried to talk them into staying in school. Interestingly, 64.4% of parents reported that it was their children's own decision, while 69.3% of parents said that they were upset. The results indicated that only a small percentage of parents offered outside counseling (9.5%), called a school counselor (22.8%), or called the child's teachers (26.1%) (see Table 2).

Regarding the use of time, a majority of gifted dropouts (73.8%) responded that they never or rarely used a computer, not including playing video/computer games, and only 5.9% of them responded that they used a computer every day. Also, 37% of gifted dropouts responded that they never or rarely spent their time doing their hobbies. A large majority of dropouts (83%) responded that they never or rarely spent time volunteering.

Research Question 2

A chi-square analysis using SPSS and SUDAAN was conducted to examine the difference between gifted dropout and nongifted dropout students with respect to their plan to return to school. Prior to the analysis, the adequacy of expected frequencies was examined, and no violation of assumptions was found. The results indicated that there was no significant difference between gifted dropouts and nongifted dropouts with respect to their plan to return to school, c^2 (1, $N = 839$) = .02, $p = .88$. Only 35.85% of gifted dropouts planned to return to school, while 64.15% of gifted dropouts had no plans to return to school. Similarly, 34.87% of nongifted dropouts planned to return to school, while 65.13% of nongifted dropouts had no plans to return to school.

Table 2   Numbers and Percentages of Responses by Parents to Their Children's Decision to Drop Out (Gifted Dropouts)

Parents' Reactions	n	%
Offered to arrange outside counseling.	31	9.5
Called school counselor.	74	22.8
Called my principal/teachers.	85	26.1
Told me it was my decision.	210	64.4
Punished me for leaving school.	41	12.7
Told me they were upset.	226	69.3
Told me it was OK to leave.	44	13.5
Tried to talk me into staying in school.	247	75.8
Offered to help with personal problems.	154	47.5
Offered to help me make up missed work.	99	30.4
Offered special tutoring.	48	14.8
Offered to put me in a special program.	55	16.9
Offered to send me to another school.	98	30.3

Note: Sum of the percentages is not equal to 100 because dropouts responded either "yes" or "no" on each item. N = 334.

STUDY 2

Research Questions

1. What are the descriptive characteristics of gifted dropouts regarding their personal background (SES, race, fathers' highest level of education, mothers' highest level of education)?

2. To what extent and in what manner can variation in the dropping out of gifted students vary among students by personal and educational factors (SES, race, gender, quality of school, fathers' highest levels of education, mothers' highest levels of education, students' educational aspirations, pregnancy or child-rearing, and absenteeism)?

Sample of the Study

The sample in Study 2 consists of gifted dropout and gifted nondropout students who were eighth graders in 1988 and participated in all four rounds of student questionnaires. It should be noted that gifted dropouts in Study 1 and Study 2 are not exactly the same group because some of the gifted dropouts in Study 1 might have returned to school before the third follow-up, classifying them as nondropouts in Study 2. Also, some of the gifted dropouts in Study 1 did not participate in the third follow-up survey, thus decreasing N size in the third follow-up in 1994. Among 12,625 students who participated in the four rounds of student questionnaires, a total of 3,520 gifted students were identified as a sample using the same definition of gifted as Study 1. In Study 2, dropout

Table 3   Dropout and Gifted Status of Study 2

	Nongifted		Gifted		Total	
	n	(%)	n	(%)	N	(%)
Nondropout	8,628	(68.3%)	3,343	(26.5%)	11,971	(94.8%)
Dropout	477	(3.8%)	177	(1.4%)	654	(5.2%)
Total	9,105	(72.1%)	3,520	(27.9%)	12,625	(100.0%)

Note. The n size is unweighted.

students were defined as students who were not graduates or GED/certificate holders in 1994. The dropout and gifted status of the sample is described in Table 3.

DATA ANALYSES AND RESULTS

Research Question 1

Several descriptive data analyses were conducted to obtain general characteristics of gifted dropouts who were not graduates or GED/certificate holders in 1994. Four descriptive analyses were conducted regarding (1) percentages of gifted dropouts by SES, (2) percentages of gifted dropouts by race, (3) percentages of gifted dropouts by fathers' highest levels of education, and (4) percentages of gifted dropouts by mothers' highest levels of education.

The results indicated that almost half of the gifted dropout students (48.18%) were in the lowest quartile SES level, while only 3.56% of them were in the highest quartile SES level. By comparison, looking at gifted nondropout students, 19.97% of them were in the lowest quartile level of SES, while 33.77% of them were in the highest quartile level of SES. In a further analysis, a significant difference was found between dropout status and SES level, c^2 (3, $N = 3,021$) = 69.15, $p < .0001$. Examination of the standardized residuals indicated that more gifted dropout students were in the lowest SES level than expected, and fewer gifted dropout students were in the highest SES level than expected. On the other hand, fewer gifted nondropout students were in the lowest SES level than expected.

Secondly, ethnic and racial information about gifted dropouts was investigated and compared with gifted nondropout students. Among five categories of race in the NELS:88, 42.90% of gifted dropout students in the sample were White, 17.88% were Hispanic, 27.01% were Black, 10.45% were Native American, and 1.76% were Asian/Pacific Islanders. A chi-square analysis was performed to investigate a significant difference among racial groups with respect to their dropout status, c^2 (4, $N = 3,513$) = 9.84, $p < .04$. A significant difference was found among racial groups with respect to dropout status. The standardized residuals indicated that more Hispanic and Native Americans than expected dropped out of school, whereas fewer White and Asian Americans than expected dropped out of school.

Finally, parents' highest levels of education were examined among gifted dropout students. For fathers, a high percentage did not finish high school (39.99%) or completed high school, but did not go on to higher education (22.99%). The descriptive analysis of mothers' highest levels of education showed similar results, indicating that 25.55% of mothers of gifted dropout students did not graduate from high school, and 35.92% of them graduated only from high school. Chi-square analyses were conducted between gifted dropout and gifted nondropout students with respect to parents' highest levels of education. Significant differences were found on both fathers' educational level, c^2 (7, N = 3,458) = 48.45, p < .0001, and mothers' educational level, c^2 (7, N = 3,489) = 48.07, p <.0001. Examination of the standardized residuals indicated that more gifted dropout students' parents did not finish high school than expected, and fewer gifted dropout students' parents continued on to higher education than expected.

Research Question 2

A logistic regression analysis was conducted to examine the relationship between the criterion variable and the set of predictors. Before conducting the logistic regression data analyses, plausible range of data, missing values, outliers, and adequacy of expected frequencies were examined. As a result of the data screening, four predictors were excluded from the data analysis because of missing data on the gifted dropouts. These predictors were students' self-concept, grade-point average, standardized test scores, and extracurricular activities.

After the data screening, to find the best model, direct logistic regression analyses were performed with student group membership (gifted dropouts vs. gifted nondropouts) as a criterion variable and a set of predictors. When examining the decision to drop out by gifted students, a test of the final full model with nine predictors (SES, gender, race, students' educational aspirations, fathers' highest education level, mothers' highest education level, pregnancy or having children, school quality, and absenteeism) against a constant-only model was found to be statistically significant, c^2 (31, N = 1,505) = 332.45, p < .001. The regression coefficients, Wald statistics, odds ratio, and 95% confidence intervals of the odds ratios for each predictor are summarized in Table 4. The results indicated that, overall, five variables significantly predict gifted students' dropout behavior: students' educational aspirations (F = 8.60, p < .0001), pregnancy or child-rearing (F = 6.15, p < .01), gender (F = 9.87, p < .01), father's highest level of education (F = 12.86, p < .0001), and mother's highest level of education (F = 3.52, p < .01). In addition, SES could be considered a significant variable at the p = .07 level. Examination of the odds ratios reveals the influence of the significant variables. The odds ratio represents "the ratio of the predicted odds of dropping out with a one-unit increase in the independent variable to the predicted odds without the one-unit increase" (Rumberger, 1995, pp. 600–603). Therefore, an odds ratio that is greater than one means that the odds of dropping out increase due to a one-unit increase in the independent variable, while an odds ratio that is less than one means that the odds of dropping out decrease due to a one-unit increase in the independent variable.

The results revealed first that gifted students who wanted to finish college had significantly lower odds of dropping out of school than other students. Second, gifted students who did not have a child had significantly lower odds of dropping out of school than gifted students who had a child or were expecting a child. Third, gifted male students were about three times more likely to drop out of school than gifted female students. Fourth, White gifted students were significantly less likely to drop out than other ethnic groups. Fifth, gifted students with fathers who did not finish high school were about three times more likely to drop out of school, while gifted students with fathers who had a master's degree were significantly less likely to drop out. Interestingly, gifted students with mothers who did not finish high school or had graduated junior college were less likely to drop out. These results indicated that fathers' highest level of education was more related to gifted students' dropping out behavior than mothers' level of education. Finally, the results showed that SES was one of the important predictors of dropping out. Gifted students who were in the low quartile and medium-low quartile of SES were much more likely to drop out of high school (see Table 4).

DISCUSSION

Implications

Previous research studies have found various factors that predict which students might drop out of high school. These studies have certain limitations. First, few research studies have focused directly on the gifted dropouts using a broad definition of gifted. Most previous studies of gifted dropouts have focused on the gifted based on IQ scores. However, in the school setting, there are many talented students who are not included in this category but are potentially at risk of dropping out of school. Because this study used an existing self-report survey, nonintellective factors like motivation could not be addressed to the extent that we would have liked. However, using broad and flexible criteria, this study obtained general characteristics of gifted dropouts. A second limitation of previous studies is related to the generalization issue. Previous research studies used data that represent specific regions or schools. As the literature indicated, because school quality and personal background such as SES and ethnicity affect students' dropping out of school, national data should be used to obtain a more precise picture of high school students' dropout behavior. Using nationally representative longitudinal data, this study obtained comprehensive information about gifted dropouts not to determine the number of

Table 4   Logistic Regression Analysis of Variables Predicting Gifted Students'
Decision to Drop Out of School

Predictor Variables	Beta coeff.	T-test, B =0	Odds Ratio	95% confidence interval for odds ratio	
				Lower	Upper
Educational Aspiration					
Won't finish high school	1.08	1.25	2.95	0.54	16.07
Will finish high school	0.97	2.00?	2.63	1.02	6.78
VOC, TRD, BUS school	−0.29	−0.62	0.75	0.31	1.85
Attend college	−0.24	−.048	0.79	0.29	2.10
Finish college	−1.93	−4.23***	0.15	0.06	0.36
Continue education after college	0.00	—	1.00	1.00	1.00
Pregnancy or Having a Child					
Yes	−0.03	-0.04	0.97	0.22	4.36
No	−1.49	−2.33*	0.23	0.06	0.79
No, but expecting	0.00	—	1.00	1.00	1.00
Gender					
Male	1.05	3.14**	2.86	1.48	5.51
Female	0.00	—	1.00	1.00	1.00
Race					
Asian/Pacific Islanders	−1.51	-1.81	0.22	0.04	1.13
Hispanic	−0.63	-0.85	0.53	0.12	2.30
Black	−0.66	-0.09	0.52	0.13	2.12
White	−1.26	-2.01*	0.28	0.08	0.97
Native American	0.00	—	1.00	1.00	1.00
Quality of School SES					
Low Quartile	4.47	2.20**	87.52	1.63	4695.20
Medium low Quartile	3.86	1.90*	47.52	0.88	2579.84
Medium high Quartile	4.00	1.92*	54.42	0.90	3273.85
High Quartile	0.00	—	1.00	1.00	1.00
Absenteeism					
None	−0.61	−0.99	0.54	0.16	1.83
1 to 2 days	−0.69	−1.12	0.50	0.15	1.69
3 or 4 days	−0.42	−0.57	0.66	0.16	2.79
5 to 10 days	0.00	—	1.00	1.00	1.00
More than 10 days	0.00	—	1.00	1.00	1.00
Father's Educational Level					
Did not finish high school	1.21	2.07*	3.35	1.07	10.49
Graduated high school	−0.21	−0.35	0.81	0.25	2.65
Junior college	−1.43	−1.20	0.24	0.02	2.48
College < 4 yrs	0.80	1.34	2.22	0.69	7.16
Graduated college	−0.06	−0.07	0.94	0.17	0.03
Master's degree	−5.30	−5.68***	0.01	0.00	1.00
Ph.D., M.D. etc.	0.00	—	1.00	1.00	1.00
Mother's Education Level					
Did not finish high school	1.47	−2.45*	0.23	0.07	0.75
Graduated high school	−0.78	−1.48	0.46	0.16	1.25
Junior college	−2.44	−2.54*	0.09	0.01	0.58
College < 4 yrs	0.57	0.96	1.77	0.55	5.70
Graduated college	−0.97	−1.37	0.38	0.09	1.52
Master's degree	0.85	0.59	2.33	0.14	38.20
Ph.D., M. D. etc.	0.00	—	1.00	1.00	1.00

*$p < .05$.
**$p < .01$.
***$p < .001$.

gifted dropouts, but to help them to continue their education. More specifically, the focus was on exploring personal and educational factors related to their dropout behavior.

Several characteristics of gifted dropouts were found in this study. First, study results confirmed that many gifted dropouts were from low-SES families and racial minority groups; had parents with low levels of education; and participated less in extracurricular activities. The present study findings indicated that Hispanic and Native American students were more likely to drop out of school, while White gifted students were less likely to drop out than other ethnic groups. In addition, the study results clearly indicated that SES and parents' educational levels were significantly related to gifted students' dropping out of high school. Almost half of the gifted dropouts (48.180%) were in the lowest quartile SES level, and only 3.56% of them were in the highest quartile SES level. This number was the reverse of that for gifted nondropouts. Also, a high percentage of gifted dropouts' parents did not finish high school or only graduated from high school. The SES and parents' educational levels may relate to the educational support at home. Ekstrom and his colleagues (Ekstrom, Goertz, Pollack, & Rock, 1986) reported that (1) dropouts received fewer educational aids from parents, (2) their parents had lower educational expectations, and (3) their parents had less interest in and were less likely to monitor their children's school activities. It is not clear from this study that gifted dropouts' parents provided poor educational support to their children. However, the present study reveals that many gifted dropouts had very limited experience with computers and spent little time on hobbies. The study also shows that gifted dropouts' parents were not actively involved in their children's dropping out. Although 75% of parents tried to talk them into staying in school, only a small percentage of parents took actions such as calling the school counselor or teacher, offering special tutoring or programs, or offering another school. Although a large percentage of parents were "upset" about the decision to drop out, it is clear that more positive action should be considered on the part of parents. This result implies that potential gifted dropouts' parents should have more involvement with regard to their children's problems and communicate closely with teachers because parents' educational aspirations and their involvement may affect gifted students' performance, as well as deportment (Ekstrom et al., 1986).

Second, the finding with respect to reasons for leaving school suggests that many of the gifted students left school because they were failing school, did not like school, got a job, or were pregnant, although there were many other related reasons. Especially, school-related reasons such as "I did not like school" or "I am failing school" were common reasons among both male and female groups. This finding was similar to the previous study from NCES, which included all ability groups. According to the NCES report (1994b), the reasons for leaving school reported by dropouts were more often school-related than job-related or family-related. Also, male dropouts were more likely than female dropouts to report leaving because of school expulsion and suspension. In addition, present study results indicated that students' educational aspirations were significantly related to gifted students dropping out of school. Some gifted students have low educational aspirations because of personal or school-related problems. This suggests that teachers and parents should guide and encourage potential dropouts to continue their education.

Based on the study findings, the following recommendations for action would help potential gifted dropouts to continue their education: (1) Schools and teachers need to recognize the characteristics of gifted dropouts and identify potential gifted dropouts in the early grades; (2) school culture should be changed to meet the needs of potential gifted dropouts, providing an appropriate and challenging curriculum that addresses their particular interests and learning styles; (3) more opportunities for extracurricular activities and encouragement to participate in them should be provided to potential gifted dropouts; (4) counseling services and special programs should be given to minority and economically disadvantaged gifted students; and (5) schools and teachers should communicate closely with potential gifted dropouts' parents, and parents should have more involvement with regard to their children's problems.

It should also be noted that some of the gifted students dropped out of school because they failed their courses, even though they were identified as gifted. This finding has an important implication for teachers and researchers. In this study, we used a flexible definition that included a broad range of gifted students. If educators and researchers use a restrictive definition of giftedness, focusing on IQ only, some talented young students who are potential dropouts will be overlooked and not provided with appropriate educational assistance, such as counseling services. Therefore, it is more appropriate to use a broad definition of giftedness when we study the population of dropouts.

Limitations

One limitation that should be noted is that, in Study 2, students who participated in all four rounds of the data survey were selected as a sample, which reduced the sample size. The number of participants in NELS:88 third follow-up data was much fewer than that of other years because it is hard to follow-up with students after they graduate high school. In addition, there were many missing data points on the specific variables, especially on the gifted dropout site. For example, several variables such as self-concept, grade-point average, and standardized test scores were excluded in the data analysis in Study 2 because of missing data on the gifted dropout site. In the case of grade-point average and standardized test scores, many data on gifted dropouts were not available because they dropped out in the 12th grade. It is not clear why more gifted dropouts than gifted nondropouts have missing data on the self-concept variable. Although the literature suggested that these variables are related to the decision to drop out, it was deemed useless to include these variables in this study because of the number of missing data points.

Suggestions for Future Research

Some researchers argue that it is necessary to distinguish among the varying types of dropout behaviors. Tinto (1975) distinguished between academic dismissal and voluntary withdrawal, pointing out that academic dismissal is most closely associated with grade performance and voluntary withdrawal is not. According to Tinto, academic dismissals have low aptitudes, intellectual ability, and social status, whereas voluntary withdrawals are more likely to have high intellectual ability and high social status. Voss, Wendling, and Elliott (1966) also distinguished three major types of dropouts: involuntary dropouts, retarded dropouts, and capable dropouts. They explained that involuntary dropouts leave school because of some personal crisis, such as the death of a parent or an accident. The retarded dropouts are those who failed to do the necessary work or the requirements for graduation. Students in this category lack the ability to do the required work or have the potential ability, but lack the requisite skills. The capable dropout is the student who has the requisite ability and does superior work in school, but may or may not be making satisfactory academic progress. These students leave school for reasons other than low ability. Although these arguments did not directly focus on gifted dropouts, the finding of the present study partly supports these arguments. On the question regarding the reasons they leave school, some gifted dropouts responded that they failed school, while others responded that they left school voluntarily. It is not clear in this study that these two groups are absolutely separate; however, it is important to examine the types of gifted dropouts in the future because intervention would be different based on the reasons for dropping out. Therefore, further study is needed about the types of gifted dropouts regarding how their background and dropout patterns are different from each other.

These studies focused on exploring general characteristics of gifted dropouts and examining personal and educational factors related to their dropout decision. However, the process of dropping out is a longitudinal process, and these factors interact with each other. Therefore, it is suggested that further research should examine not only important factors, but also their causal relationship and interactions using a longitudinal path analysis technique. Also, it is suggested that further study should develop instruments or behavior check lists that identify the potential gifted dropouts. These can provide a more practical guideline to teachers and school counselors.

REFERENCES

Bachman, J., Green, S., & Wirtinen, I. (1972). Dropping out is a symptom. *Education Digest, 37,* 1–5.

Barr, R. B., & Knowles, G.W. (1986). *The San Diego city schools 1984–85 school leaver and high school diploma program participant attitude study.* San Diego, CA: San Diego City Schools: Planning, Research and Evaluation Division.

Beacham, H. C. (1980). *Reaching and helping high school dropouts and potential school leavers*. Tallahassee, FL: Florida A&M University. (ERIC Document Reproduction Service No. ED 236451)

Bernoff, L. (1981). *Report of Indiana public school dropout-graduate prediction study*. South Bend, IN: Indiana University, South Bend School of Education.

Betts, G. T., & Neihart, M. (1988). Profiles of the gifted and talented, *Gifted Child Quarterly, 32*, 248–253.

Bracey, G. W. (1994). Dropping in on dropping out. *Phi Delta Kappan, 75*, 726–727.

Cervantes, L. (1965). *The dropout: Causes and cures*. Ann Arbor, MI: The University of Michigan Press.

Cordy, T. A. (1993). *Leaving: A quantitative and qualitative case study of an urban dropout problem*. Unpublished doctoral dissertation. The University of Connecticut, Storrs.

Curtis, J., McDonald, J., Doss, J., & Davis, W. (1983). *Dropout prediction*. Austin, TX: Texas Office of Research and Evaluation. (ERIC Document Reproduction Service No. ED 233282)

Davis, H. (1984). Self-concept profiles of gifted underachievers. (Doctoral dissertation, University of Rochester, 1983). *Dissertation Abstracts International, 45*(04), 1072. (University Microfilms International No. AAC84-13056)

Ekstrom, R. B., Goertz, M. E., Pollack, J. M., & Rock, D. A. (1986). Who drops out of high school and why? Findings from a national study. *Teachers College Record, 87*, 356–373.

Frazer, L. H. (1992). *The use of school-maintained and school-related variables to differentiate between students who stay in and students who drop out of high school*. Unpublished doctoral dissertation, The University of Texas, Austin.

Hertz, D. (1989). *Learning styles and high school dropouts*. Unpublished doctoral dissertation. Laurentian University of Sudbury, Ontario, Canada.

Hewitt, J. D., & Johnson, W. S. (1979). Dropping out in Middletown. *The High School Journal, 62*, 252–256.

Irvine, D. J. (1987). What research doesn't show about gifted dropouts. *Educational Leadership, 44*, 79–80.

Johnson, D. E. (1970). Personality characteristics in relation to college persistence. *Journal of Counseling Psychology, 17*, 162–167.

Keith, T. Z., & Benson, M. J. (1992). Effects of manipulable influences on high school grades across five ethnic groups. *Journal of Educational Research, 86*, 85–93.

Kunkel, M. A., Pittman, A. M., Curry, E. W., Hildebrand, S. K., & Walling, D. D. (1991). Attrition patterns in a summer program for gifted junior high students. *Roeper Review, 14*, 90–93.

Lajoie, S. P., & Shore, B. M. (1981). Three myths? The overrepresentation of the gifted among dropouts, delinquents, and suicides. *Gifted Child Quarterly, 25*, 138–143.

Lobosco, A. (1992). *Individual, school, and community correlates of high school graduation*. Unpublished doctoral dissertation, University of Illinois, Chicago.

Martin, D. L., Jr. (1981). *Identifying potential dropouts: A research report*. Frankfort, KY: Kentucky State Department of Education. (ERIC Document Reproduction Service No. ED 216304)

Massey, S. R., & Crosby, J. (1982). *Study of George Valley high school dropout program*. Scarborough, ME: New England Institute of Education. (ERIC Document Reproduction Service No. ED 220768)

National Center for Education Statistics. (1983). *High school dropouts: Descriptive information from high school and beyond*. Washington, DC: U.S. Government Printing Office.

National Center for Education Statistics. (1993). Dropout rates in the United States: 1992. (NCES 94-464). Washington, DC: U.S. Government Printing Office.

National Center for Education Statistics (1994a). *National education longitudinal study of 1988: Second follow-up: Student component data file user's manual.* (NCES 94-374). Washington, DC: U.S. Government Printing Office.

National Center for Education Statistics (1994b). *Dropout rates in the United States: 1993.* (NCES 94-669). Washington, DC: U.S. Government Printing Office.

National Center for Education Statistics (1997). *Dropout rates in the United States: 1996.* (NCES 98-250). Washington, DC: U.S. Government Printing Office.

Noth, N., & O'Neill, B. (1981). *Dropout identification: A preliminary study of the Pasco School District.* (ERIC Document Reproduction Service No. ED215013)

Renzulli, J. S. (1986). The three-ring conception of giftedness: A developmental model for creative productivity. In R. J. Sternberg & F. Davidson (Eds.), *Conceptions of giftedness* (pp. 53–92). Cambridge, London: Cambridge University Press.

Research Triangle Institute. (1995). *SUDAAN, release 7.0: Software for statistical analysis of correlated data.* Research Triangle Park, NC: Author.

Robertson, E. (1991). Neglected dropouts: The gifted and talented. *Equity & Excellence, 25,* 62–74.

Roderick, M. R. (1991). *The path to dropping out among public school youth: Middle school and early high school experiences.* Unpublished doctoral dissertation, Harvard University, Cambridge, MA.

Rumberger, R. W. (1981). *Why kids drop out of schools.* Paper presented at the annual meeting of the America Educational Research Association, Los Angeles, CA.

Rumberger, R. W. (1995). Dropping out of middle school: A multilevel analysis of students and schools. *American Educational Research Journal, 32,* 583–25.

Sadowski, A. J. (1987). A case study of the experiences of and influences upon gifted high school dropouts. *Dissertation Abstracts International, 48*(04), 893. (University Microfilms International No. AAC87-16185)

Schreiber, D. (1979). Dropout causes and consequences. In M. C. Alkin (Ed.), *The encyclopedia of educational research* (4th ed.; pp. 308–316). Toronto, Ontario, Canada: Macmillan.

Sewell, T. E., Palmo, A. J., & Manni, J. L. (1981). High school dropout: Psychological, academic, and vocational factors. *Urban Education, 16,* 65–76.

Solorzano, L. (1983, August). Now, gifted children get some breaks. *U.S. News & World Report, 8,* 32.

Soltys, T. V. (1990). *A study of predictor variables as indicators of potential high school dropouts.* Unpublished doctoral dissertation, Temple University, Phildelphia, PA.

Stephenson, R. S. (1985). *A study of the longitudinal dropout rate: 1980 eighth-grade cohort followed from June, 1980 through February, 1985.* Miami, FL: Dade County Public Schools Office of Educational Accountability.

Thornburg, H. D. (1975). Attitudinal determinants in holding dropouts in school. *Journal of Educational Research, 68,* 181–185.

Tinto, V. (1975). Dropout from higher education: A theoretical synthesis of recent research. *Review of Educational Research, 45,* 89–125.

Tinto, V. (1982). Limits of theory and practice in student attrition. *Journal of Higher Education, 53,* 687–700.

Tinto, V. (1988). Stages of student departure. Reflections on the longitudinal character of student leaving. *Journal of Higher Education, 59,* 438–455.

U.S. Department of Education. (1993). *National excellence: A case for developing America's talent*. Washington, DC: U.S. Government Printing Office.

Vaughan, R. P. (1968). College dropouts: Dismissed vs. withdrawn. *Personnel and Guidance Journal, 46,* 685–689.

Voss, H. L., Wendling, A., & Elliott, D. S. (1966). Some types of high school dropouts. *Journal of Educational Research, 59,* 363–368.

Watson, C. (1976). *Focus on dropouts*. Toronto, Ontario, Canada: Ontario Institute for Studies in Education.

Willett, J. B., & Singer, J. D. (1991). From whether to when: New methods for studying student dropout and teacher attrition. *Review of Educational Research, 61,* 407–450.

Young, V., & Reich, C. (1974). *Patterns of dropping out*. Toronto, Ontario, Canada: Toronto Board of Education Research.

Zaccaria, L., & Creaser, J. (1971). Factors related to persistence in an urban commuter university. *Journal of College and Student Personnel, 12,* 286–291.

Index

Note: References to tables or figures are indicated by *italic type* and the addition of "*t*" or "*f*" respectively.

**CORWIN
PRESS**

The Corwin Press logo—a raven striding across an open book—represents the union of courage and learning. Corwin Press is committed to improving education for all learners by publishing books and other professional development resources for those serving the field of K–12 education. By providing practical, hands-on materials, Corwin Press continues to carry out the promise of its motto: **"Helping Educators Do Their Work Better."**